Enneagram Relationships

Using the Enneagram to Find a Form of Prayer
That Works for You

(Working With Subtypes of the Awareness to
Action Enneagram)

Claude Shaw

Published by Knowledge Icons

Claude Shaw

All Rights Reserved

Enneagram Relationships: Using the Enneagram to Find a Form of Prayer That Works for You (Working With Subtypes of the Awareness to Action Enneagram)

ISBN 978-1-990084-47-8

All rights reserved. No part of this guide may be reproduced in any form without permission in writing from the publisher except in the case of brief quotations embodied in critical articles or reviews.

Legal & Disclaimer

The information contained in this book is not designed to replace or take the place of any form of medicine or professional medical advice. The information in this book has been provided for educational and entertainment purposes only.

The information contained in this book has been compiled from sources deemed reliable, and it is accurate to the best of the Author's knowledge; however, the Author cannot guarantee its accuracy and validity and cannot be held liable for any errors or omissions. Changes are periodically made to this book. You must consult your doctor or get professional medical advice before using any of the suggested remedies, techniques, or information in this book.

Upon using the information contained in this book, you agree to hold harmless the Author from and against any damages, costs, and expenses, including any legal fees potentially resulting from the application of any of the information provided by this guide. This disclaimer applies to any damages or injury caused by the use and application, whether directly or indirectly, of any advice or information presented, whether for breach of contract, tort, negligence, personal injury, criminal intent, or under any other cause of action.

You agree to accept all risks of using the information presented inside this book. You need to consult a professional medical practitioner in order to ensure you are both able and healthy enough to participate in this program.

Table of Contents

INTRODUCTION 1

CHAPTER 1: STRUCTURE 5

CHAPTER 2: DON'T BE AFRAID TO KNOW YOURSELF 17

CHAPTER 3: UNDERSTANDING THE ENNEAGRAM 31

CHAPTER 4: HUMANS, A NEVER-ENDING STORY 44

CHAPTER 5: THE HISTORY OF ENNEAGRAM 55

CHAPTER 6: BUILDING SELF-UNDERSTANDING 63

CHAPTER 7: THE ENNEAGRAM 76

CHAPTER 8: HOW CAN YOU FIGURE OUT WHAT KIND OF PERSONALITY YOU ARE? 89

CHAPTER 9: ENNEAGRAM TEST 100

CHAPTER 10: EMPATHS AND RELATIONSHIPS 106

CHAPTER 11: ENNEA-TYPE FOUR – "THE INDIVIDUALIST" 123

CHAPTER 12: ENNEAGRAM TYPE 3 - THEPERFORMER/ACHIEVER 138

CHAPTER 13: THE POINT SEVEN ARCHETYPE: THE ENTHUSIAST 150

CHAPTER 14: TYPE FIVE - THE INVESTIGATOR 164

CHAPTER 15: FIND A NEW JOB WITH ENNEAGRAM AND BECOME A GREAT LEADER 177

CONCLUSION 184

Introduction

Ever since the concept first gained popularity, and as we all continue to understand it through the years, Emotional Intelligence has been growing away from being a mere "idea" to becoming a concrete facet of human behavior. Like any muscle in the body, emotional intelligence has become increasingly important to exercise and develop in our hopes of becoming better individuals. Yet, for many, the question still looms large: What is emotional intelligence?

In this book, you will not only begin to answer that important question by understanding the roles that our emotions, thoughts, and habits play into the development of emotional intelligence (EI). Learn all the important elements of this human ability and there you can glean the answer to the much bigger question of how to improve your emotional intelligence.

I'm sure that not a few will agree that this significant ability to recognize, understand, and eventually manage one's emotions has become a crucial part of daily living. The web of human emotions can be quite complex and tricky to navigate in the aim of establishing positive human interactions in the various areas of our lives. I, for one, have grown to be particularly interested in EI the moment my now-5-year-old son started preschool. I felt that the pressure to raise a well-adjusted, confident, and admirable boy was more for me, having studied Psychology all my adult life. Learning does not end, does it? And this is why I endeavored to uncover more about the subject as I intend to guide my young son through the intricate web of human emotions as early as I can manage.

The best part of educating myself more about emotional intelligence, beyond being a tenable model to my child, is that I myself am able to improve my own attitude in the relationships I have; I have become more confident in taking on leadership roles at work; and I learned to be more systematic in preserving harmony, even initiating positive changes all around.

There is a multitude of reasons for you to learn and grow along with me. Are you, like me, raising small children? Have you reached a point in your career wherein you feel ready, but are quite hesitant, to take on bigger responsibilities in your career? Do you hit a few similar bumps again and again in your personal relationships that you just can't seem to avoid? If there is even just one "yes" in there, trust me – you should not wait a minute more in acquainting yourself more deeply with your emotional intelligence.

The scientific research you will read in this book will take you steps closer to understanding the variance between individuals with high and low emotional intelligence and on which rung on the EI spectrum you most likely fall. Allow this book to help you become a more self-aware, empathic, and motivated individual. And then witness the unfolding of a better you at the heart of all those you hold dear and true.

Chapter 1: Structure

We describe the foundation of Enneagram, and its nine character types or enterotypes, to validate its improvement in people and its use in coaching. We noticed that the identification of our enneastyle based mainly on Enneagram is quite misleading. From what we have learned, we suggest a way to find out in a simple way, the personality type according to the Enneagram.

Enneagram, the effigy of nine personality types or enterotypes, is broadly used in the development of people. This is the reason why we have decided to include it in this collection of articles on teaching tools. Like other cases, we will understand its foundation and assess its suitability to be used in coaching and people development.

One of the functions of the Enneagram is to raise awareness of yourself and from there to promote development. The same component we find in neuroscience, but with a significant difference. At NeuroQuotient® we no longer deal with personality, only with behavior, and with the foundation of his brain (neuro-behavior).

The instruments we mentioned in earlier posts have simple fashions that dictate them. William M. in relation to DISC. Marston's effigy. Carl Jung's theory using the Myers-Briggs Ladies in MBTI. And also the psychological work of cognition of Carl Jung through the Lothian Lords, in Insights Discovery.

In the case of the enneagram, it is very inconvenient to answer the question.

With whom do each of the nine character types of the Enneagram identify?

So that we can analyze the basics of Enneagram, we will focus on two first-rate experts: Richard Risso and David Daniels. From his works:

Enigma of the Wisdom: The Complete Guide to the Psychological and Spiritual Growth for the Nine Personality Types - via Don Richard Risso and via Don Richard Risso

The Essential Enneagram: The Definitive Personality Test and Self Discovery Guide - David Daniels, Virginia Price. HarperCollins eBook

We chose them, due to the fact that both Risso-Hudson and Daniel-Price tried to facilitate the identification of the personality type, antitype, in the Enneagram. We agree that Riso-Hudson specifically with his questionnaire TRIE (in the Rapid Test of Idenogram).

Anyway, to solve our personality type detection situation according to the enneagram, we will think about an alternative system. We will see this later.

Origin of the Enneagram. The nine-character model sorts or animates.

Risso and Hudson tell us that we should distinguish the Enneagram symbol from the nine personality types.

The symbol is part of the traditions that upheld the religions of Judaism, Christianity, and Islam. This picture is made up of three parts: circle, triangle, and hexagon.

Enneagram nine personality types
Fig.1.

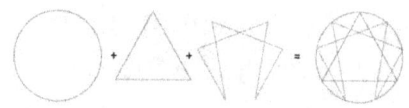

Enneagram symbol is the result of a combination of the circle, equilateral triangle, and hexagram.

The introducer of the image in the modern world was once George Ivanovich Gurdjieff (1875). Along with his friends tried to learn more about ancient traditions. They

Named himself ers Seekers After Truth '(S.A.T.).

The most recent treatment was used by Oscar Ichajo and, above all, by his disciple Claudio Naranjo (Valparaiso, Chile), a psychiatrist at Gestalt Current.

In the seventies, Naranjo worked with a panel of people to reinforce every type of symptom. Defining the characteristics of each of the 9 character types. This Naranjo work clears the Enneagram from most esotericism that he could initially reflect.

Claudio Naranjo designed and developed the program S.A.T. The reason for this is to raise a psycho-spiritual assignment that embraces both therapeutic and contemplative aspects. In the therapeutic aspect, it is based entirely on an in-depth investigation of infant conditioning through the psychology of types. He retained the identity of (S.A.T., Seekers After Truth).

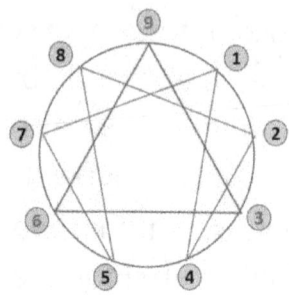

Each person types in anagram symbol and some structure is from ads triads or centers.

To be reliable for our purpose, to make the complex inexpensive, we will begin by way of setting 9 numbers on the symbol of the anagram. (Line number 2)

The triangle has 9 at the apex and three and 6 at the base. There are 3 on the right and 6 on the left. A number of the remaining nine personality types are deployed on the hexagram. Starting 1 to the right of 9 and continuing clockwise. The 9 character types of enneagram are correlated between 1 and 9 on the circle.

Enneagram nine personality types

The nine personality types of anagrams or antitypes are numbered 1 to 9. 9, 3, 6 are located at the corner of the triangle, resting in these hexagrams. 1 to 9 on the circle following the clock hands.

The ads that are in-between types 9, 3 and 6 are known as triads or centers'. Each 'triad' character type is included anterior and posterior.

The first step to development, remembering, is awareness. These triads or centers have an essential role in this route. They are based entirely on the three centers of the human psyche: instinct, emotion and thought. They focus on doing, feeling and thinking, respectively. It is indeed worth remembering that in neuro patients, when we talk about neuro-behaviors, we are referring to doing, questioning, and feeling like a whole, and their cerebral foundations.

Personal improvement is very deep with Engram. Once we have identified our knowledge base, the possibilities of self-awareness that we can collect are very valuable. However, the first step, determining our personality type in Enneagram, is complex. This is due to the lack of simple infrastructure.

But, in this weblog, we are looking for more practicality than transit and we have tried to simplify this selection. We believe that this is feasible to do with the DISC model and the so-called social styles or Hornevian groups of the nine personality types of The Enneagram.

We will explore a quick description of each of the Enneagram's 9 personality types in a published stop. But before that, we are going to create a concept of structure. From there we can extract our approximate type and in the final descriptions, we will see if it suits us extra or very little.

We can consider that the DISC mannequin is structured in a 2 × 2 table. According to Marston's model 2 × 2 = four DISC personality types are mainly based on two dimensions. 1. Understanding oneself as the most efficient or inferior (motor self) towards the environment and the environment as unfavorable or favorable (motor stimulation).

After an in-depth look at each of the 9 personality types of the Enneagram, it appears to be very

We believe the answer lies in social styles or Hornovian groups.

The Social Style or The Hornavian Group

Horniman organizations indicate the social style of each individual type and the way each person satisfies his or her dominant desires that the trio indicates.

Horniman corporations are named after Karen Horny. Horny was a psychiatrist who, beginning with Freud, recognized the three methods that people use to solve their inner complexities. These Hornavian companies additionally indicate every type of social style.

There are three styles: aggressive, withdrawn and obedient.

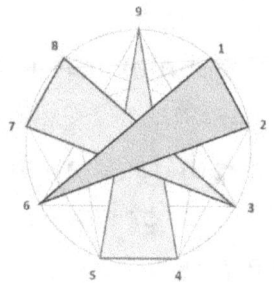

Aggressive, according to Horny, 'go against'. Faced with difficulties, they do not reappear or demand protection from various people. Does this sound like anyone who feels the environment is the most perfect, right?

The aggression group consists of 8, 7 variants (we had already placed them in the top row), and three The 3, at the apex of the purple isosceles triangle So, type three will actually be the one that is sized in the middle frame between 8 and 7.

According to Horny, crew obedient crew share the need to be useful to others. Facing difficulties, they ask themselves what is the right thing. How can I meet the expectations of others? How will be responsible?

Thinking extra about the expectations of others than your own, it is very possible that these people experience inferiorities with the environment, right?

There are types 1 and 2 in the group of complexes (we had already placed them in the back row) and 6. 6 in the upper vertex of the blue isosceles triangle (see original 5). 6 We can put between 1 and 2.

Enneagram nine-person types

Horny or social group. Karen Horny classifies 9 Ani Tipos into three groups: aggression, compliance, and withdrawal. In red, blue and green, respectively, marked in the figure

A quarterly signifies a fundamentally uncertain need. Let's look at a price in Table I of each of them and the character types of Enneagram that represent it.

Finally, we have a crew of 'evacuation'. According to Horny, they react to stress through their retreat into the world, entering an inner space. Looking at the isosceles triangle that we have left (green) with 9 in the upper (top), we can assume that 9 will coincide in the middle of the middle row. Considering also what Risso and Hudson tell us that 4 aspire to be different from the others and that they are in a way far away in social situations, we can assume that 4 will be more healthy on the left.

Then, how can we identify our hypothesized person types from social styles and the DISC model in Enneagram?

From here, the three × three sizes that we have proposed, we can try to identify their character type in the anagram by asking the following questions.

Chapter 2: Don't Be Afraid To Know Yourself

Knowing oneself is tiring and, in some cases, a little painful, but only in this way can we take the reins of our lives. Did you ever look at yourself in the mirror and not understand who the hell was that person reflected? If you often do not know why you have reached the point where you are, if you do not understand the decisions you have made, if you think your stupidity is something intolerable know that you are not stupid, you are just an individual who needs to better understand their own personality, accept it and live according to a regime of high honesty. Get rid of all the buildings, find your spaces and live free to breathe in a better world.

What do you see when you look at yourself in the mirror? Are you happy with what you see, not just on a physical level, or would you like to be a completely different person? Are you aware of how you are?

What does it mean to know yourself?

It means knowing how to stop, despite the hectic pace of everyday life, and learn to listen to each other, to read the intricacies of one's soul, the one who knows who we are, the one who hides our desires, the one who can indicate the path to follow. Soul, psyche, heart, no matter what the name you attribute to the core nucleus that characterizes you, as long as you can stop and make intimate knowledge of it. Sometimes we believe we know each other, but what we see is only a reflection of what others think and say about us. If this is perfectly normal in childhood, in adulthood it is necessary to come to terms with what we really are, looking at what is really hidden within us or we will risk acting to please others, giving them our lives.

The compelling need to change can be hidden in a tiring moment, when things do not turn, when we feel paralyzed. This is the occasion to look inside oneself, avoiding to escape introspection, throwing oneself on other activities or running aground following the advice of others, imitating their choices. Take in hand, start a deep friendship with yourself, give yourself time to deepen your knowledge of your core group, a strenuous and, in some cases, painful operation, but only in this way can we take over the reins of our lives and take paths evolutionary.

You have to know that when something goes wrong, most of us ask the wrong question ("why"), while the question that helps us take a step forward is "what?".

Instead of asking "why am I not happy at work?", Let's try to ask "what can I do to be?" In this way, we will be able not only to discover more about ourselves but also to know our capabilities.

Getting to know yourself better means having real benefits in return. What are the main ones? We list them below:

to know with more certainty what we want;

to have greater decision-making power;

to have the chance to be more creative;

being able to identify more easily the causes of our malaise;

to improve our self-esteem;

to improve the quality of our social and personal relationships.

"If you know the enemy and yourself, your victory is certain. If you know yourself but not the enemy, your chances of winning and losing are equal. If you do not know the enemy or even yourself, you will succumb in every battle », **Sun Tzu.**

Knowing oneself is the ability to investigate within oneself, to discover and understand that the essence of our life is inside, not outside of us. The great Greek philosopher Socrates has made the "know thyself" a pivotal point of his thought, indeed of the entire ancient Greece, for the good of man, so that he may become what his deepest nature demands. If we stop to reflect, to meditate, to observe ourselves, we will be able to come to discover who we are, for which it is precisely the knowledge that allows man to know himself and therefore to know what is the most suitable way to live happily.

ìWe can dare to say that the Greek sages have introduced the I into the western world and for the first time man coincides with his interiority, with his soul. But what does it mean to know oneself today, in the modern age? Knowing oneself first of all means knowing one's limits, because it is unthinkable to reach happiness if we do not accept ourselves as we are. This does not mean that we have to fossilize ourselves, but it is a fundamental starting point for embarking on an evolutionary path, of spiritual awakening, because it is precisely starting from the awareness of limits, that we can overcome them and improve ourselves. Once we have acquired this awareness, everyone can take care of what belongs to him, to do what he does best. One must follow one's vocations in order to enhance one's abilities and put them at the service of others. A just society based on "know yourself" should allow people to do what they were born for. Vocational work is the only way that allows the individual to do his work with love and passion, whatever it is.

And it is at this point that knowing oneself becomes a source of happiness, as a means to reach self-knowledge, and to travel the only path that leads to happiness. All it takes is a good dose of courage to look reality in the face and tell yourself the truth. In today's society, unfortunately, we hide too often behind ourselves because it is easier to appear than to be, and it is the same society that does not want us to be ourselves. In reality most of us are not interested at all in knowing each other, deluded as it is to already know everything. And it is in this illusion that at some point in our lives, the lack of knowing oneself leads to a total sense of loss, because we will no longer know who we really are, where we are and what we are doing here. And no external response can come to our aid.

This lack of inner security will essentially be due to an almost total unawareness of who we really are: it is as if our interaction with ourselves, with others, with our work, with our normal activities, produces only dissonances and inner voids . We feel immersed in a reality that does not belong to us, unsure of our choices and decisions, uncertain about the way forward, and we no longer know who we are and what we really want. All this causes unhappiness!

We all feel if we are good or bad, if we perceive feelings of lightness or heaviness, well-being or discomfort. The area of intimate feeling should become the place of analysis, observation, taking charge of what should be eliminated, elaborated, expanded, integrated or transformed on the basis of what is necessary to carry out in order to promote fullness expression of their own requests for fulfillment.

Human beings are not born with destructive but creative tendencies. He wishes to manifest his inner nature, as an acorn wants to become the tree that it is.

Each person is unique, since each person has a genetic datum that distinguishes him and subjective experiences that have marked him on the basis of emotional and affective imprints, both negative and positive. There is no doubt that two children (even twins) who grew up in the same family present different temperamental traits and establish completely different relational dynamics with their parents and social environment. The deepest aspiration deposited in the human being is that of manifesting one's existence, through a vision and a mission that give meaning and meaning to the fact of having come into the world. Human beings are not born with destructive but creative tendencies. He wishes to manifest his inner nature, as an acorn wants to become the tree that it is. No human being loves infidelity to his own nature, although he can betray himself and his vocation.

When this happens a profound sensation of anguish and existential emptiness arises. To become the tree that we are we need a favorable environment, where we can manifest the light of authenticity that is already present in us and which must not be purchased anywhere. When this process of revelation of one's true self is interrupted or castrated, we assume that there are disharmonies of behavior that can lead to psychosomatic manifestations, neuroses of various kinds and, in the most serious cases, psychotic states. When we decide to restore order in our disorder and take the path of homecoming, every form of discomfort begins to be cured, behaviors correct and a feeling of peace and harmony is released that grows with the passing of the healing process.

All this requires a serious commitment to work with the utmost honesty on oneself, not being afraid to meet one's inner monsters or drowning in puddles of pain frozen in the depths of forgetfulness. The fact of being able to grow does not cancel the fragility of which we are composed or the limits of which we are constituted but it integrates them with the possibilities of finding solutions, of reworking a wound, of activating new resources in order to become more and more human and to find the beauty inside and outside us in a face illuminated by faith and love for oneself, for others and for the Absolute. All this is not possible unless we understand that our decisions are what guide us towards maturity, in the lightness of a soul that makes somersaults of happiness within the sky of possibilities. The truth is that knowing yourself helps us to live better.

Try to understand why you lie and to whom. We have all told a few lies, to other people and to ourselves, and for different reasons. Developing a systematic plan to be more honest, however, will be difficult if you fail to identify these reasons and the people you lie to most often.

The lies to make a good impression include hyperboles, embellishments and inventions that we tell others, and ourselves, to make us feel better about our inadequacies. When you are unhappy for some reason, it is much easier to fill the void with lies than to tell the truth.

We tell lies to our peers that we consider better than us because we want their respect. Unfortunately, being dishonest is a lack of respect in the long run. Recognize people the ability to understand you at a deeper level.

The lies that prevent us from being embarrassed' include the lies told to hide improper behavior, transgressions or activities we are not proud of. If your mother found a pack of cigarettes in your jacket, you could lie and say that I belong to a friend of yours to avoid punishment.

We tell lies to the authority figures to avoid embarrassment and punishment. When we have done something for which we feel guilty, we tell lies to eliminate guilt and avoid punishment.

Now I want to give you a small gift to really begin to understand that knowing yourself and living according to a universal law of honesty is the best thing you can do.

Below you will find two easy exercises to do for your personal growth path. They are part of the great and wise practice of the Enneagram and allow you to have a better awareness of your whole being. Don't be afraid to start getting to know yourself, immediately start the road to your happy future.

EXERCISE # 1 - Learn the sound of your voice

It sounds crazy but none of us initially has the true knowledge of our own voice. And the voice says everything about a person, it is the most powerful tool with which humans establish a bridge with other people. Learning the sound, accepting every nuance of the tone of your voice is the first big step towards a conscious life. Take a book, a book you know very well and read aloud with a voice recorder (the one on your smartphone will do just fine) three pages every day for a week. Record your voice in the morning and then listen again in the evening. Learn to understand your tones and your vibrations.

EXERCISE # 2 - Do not lie

Even adult people are in a position to tell small lies. Even simply to look more interesting. A little tale told to the neighbor to impress him with fantastic holidays, a lie without malice so as not to make a grandmother worry. Here in this exercise I want to ask you to choose two hours a day when you don't tell lies. No lie of any kind, always and only to the truth.

To be honest with yourself is to be consistent with your thinking and acting. Sometimes it is very difficult to keep ourselves consistent, but if we succeed it means that we really know each other, we accept each other and we are satisfied with us. If this were not the case, if we lied to ourselves, how could we expect others to be sincere towards us? Whoever is not honest with himself has a strong desire to be what he is not and only by taking refuge in lies does he feel fulfilled.

Nobody likes lies. Unfortunately, being dishonest with others and ourselves is in some cases simpler than telling the truth. But it doesn't have to be this way: learning to be honest and not feeling the need to lie can help you improve your relationships and lighten your conscience. Slightly changing your perspective and choosing an honesty policy can help you not need to lie and let you tell the truth more willingly.

Chapter 3: Understanding The Enneagram

There are many personality tests in the public domain. You may have heard of some of them. The Myers Briggs personality test is one of the most famous of these, and you might have taken this yourself. But I would venture to say that The Enneagram is more than a personality test. It would be more accurately described as an immensely powerful tool for personal, not to mention collective, transformation.

So just what is this enigma known as the Enneagram? To delve a little deeper into its true meaning and origins, we are first going to examine the symbol which represents it.

What the Enneagram Figure Means

The Enneagram symbol or figure is made up of three individual shapes, each having its own separate meaning. We will first examine the underlying circle:

The Circle

It will come as no surprise that the circle represents the wholeness or oneness of life - as in the Circle of Life. The circle also serves as a kind of container within which we conduct our lives. As we navigate our way through life, fragmentation can occur, often because of the ego. The goal is to reach awareness that we have never actually lost our wholeness.

The Triangle

In many cultures, three is regarded as a mystical and magical number. This is sometimes known as the Law of Threes. This law holds that every phenomenon consists of three individual forces. When three forces are present, things start to happen. But with only one or two forces available, nothing at all happens. Each force has a different name. The first is known as the active or positive or motivating force. The second one is called the negative or passive or denying force and the third is named the neutralizing, facilitating or invisible force. As an esoteric law, the Law of Threes works both in our inner world and our outer world. You might be able to observe it in your interactions with other people.

There are numerous cultural examples of the Law of Threes. One of the most pervasive and one which the majority of people will be familiar with, is that of the concept of the holy trinity - the father, son and The Holy Spirit - which is espoused by the Christian tradition.

The Hexad

The Hexad is a more unusual and irregular symbol which finds its origins in Sufism - the mystical branch of Islam. It is actually a six pointed figure but it follows seven points, from the start, through six changes of momentum, then back to its origin, which is considered the seventh point. It represents the Law of Seven, which is sometimes known as the law of octaves. It propounds that phenomena evolves in seven steps. Along with the Law of Threes, it was believed by Gurdjieff, a chief proponent of The Enneagram, that the Law of Seven was a global law and essential to his cosmology.

The Law of Seven states that the path of movement, either towards or away from anything, does not occur in a straight line. Rather, there are periods of striving, falling and striving again - a kind of rising and falling of energies along the way.

These three shapes are overlaid onto one another in order to create the Enneagram symbol. The lines on the Enneagram symbol show a path to a richer and fuller life. Self-observation is encouraged here, in order to avoid the different triggers of our personalities which might tend to lead one astray.

The numbers - one to nine - on the Enneagram symbol, represent the nine different personality types. The relationship between the numbers are demonstrated by the lines that connect them together. Each number is only connected to two other numbers.

About the Wings

No one person is made up purely of one personality type. Everyone is a mixture of their main type together with one of the two types next to it on the Enneagram figure. Whichever adjacent type that you most identify with is known as your 'wing.'

Your dominant wing is indicated by the higher score of one of the types that exists on either side of your basic type. For example, if your basic type is Three, your wing will be Two or Four, whichever one has the highest score. It is worth noting that the second highest overall score on your Enneagram test is not necessarily that of your wing.

The idea is that the wing types have an extra influence on your basic type.

The Triads (or Centers)

The nine personality types of the Enneagram are arranged into three triads, otherwise known as centers. Three of the types are in the instinctive center (One, Eight and Nine), three in the feeling center (Two, Three and Four) and three in the thinking center, (Five, Six and Seven). The three personalities that occupy the same center share the same strengths and weaknesses as one another.

Each triad or center is associated with a particular emotion. The instinctive center is associated with anger, whereas the feeling center tends to feel more shame. And the thinking center is linked to feelings of fear. Of course, each and every person can be subject to each and every emotion, but in each triad, the personalities associated with it are especially affected by that triad's emotional theme. You'll find that each personality type has a particular way of coping with its dominant emotion.

The three numbers within each triad or center have a pattern that they follow. The first number in each triad expresses the emotion that it is hyper-focused on. So types Eight, Two and Five express and externalize their emotions. This means that Eight externalizes anger, Two externalizes shame and Five externalizes fear.

This means that they either project the emotion outwardly or experience it outside themselves. When these personalities experience these emotions, they manifest right in front of us.

The second number in each center represses the emotion upon which it focuses. That is, Nine, Three and Six. So Nine represses anger, Three represses shame and Six represses fear. In other words, they do their best to pretend that the emotion doesn't exist for them.

The third number in each center internalizes the emotion it is most associated with. Thus, One, Four and Seven try to internalize their emotions. One internalizes anger, Four internalizes shame and Seven internalizes fear. These personalities experience these emotions inwardly or turn it in on themselves. This is different from repression because they still feel the emotion they are concealing, but they are choosing not to show it. This may lead these personality types, especially Four, to brood.

How to Identify Your Personality Type

The upcoming chapters provide a comprehensive guide to the nine different personality types, set out in numerical order. Each chapter begins with a check list comprising of fifteen questions to ask yourself in order to ascertain whether or not you are likely to be that particular type.

It would be a good idea to keep a record of which personality type you tick off the most statements for. This practice should identify your personality type. In a similar way, keep track of which adjacent personality type you score the most for. This will be your dominant wing.

It is quite common to find a little of yourself in all of the nine Enneagram personality types, although one of them should stand out as being the closest to you. This is your basic type.

We are all familiar with the ongoing debate between nature and nurture. In terms of the Enneagram, experts agree that we are born with a dominant type. This inborn temperament seems to determine the ways in which we adapt to our early childhood environment.

People do not switch from one personality type to another. For instance, if you are born a One, you will stay a One for the entirety of your life. A few other points are worth bearing in mind. All the types apply equally to men and to women. And a larger number on the Enneagram scale is no better or worse than a lower number. In other words, an eight is no better than a three or vice versa. Each type has its own inherent strengths and weaknesses. No Enneagram personality type is better or worse than another. We should all strive to be our best selves rather than striving to emulate other types.

About the Levels

Of course, not all the people from the same type will be exactly the same. This is obvious when we consider the diversity of the human beings we are surrounded with. So what is it that accounts for these differences?

Each personality type is made up of nine levels of development. This hypothesis was first reached by Don Riso in 1977. Riso, together with Russ Hudson, further developed the idea in the 1990s. The concept of the levels adds depth to our understanding of the Enneagram system and accounts both for the differences that arise between people of the same type and also how people can change, positively or negatively.

The levels of development provide deeper understanding to the explanation of the different elements contained within a personality type. This ties in with the complexity of human nature. The levels of development provide for us a kind of skeletal framework which allows us to see how all the traits of a particular type are interrelated, and how a healthy trait can become average, or can become unhealthy. Of course, this can work in the opposite direction also.

The levels show us that the personality is dynamic and ever changing. It helps us understand that people can change states within their personality, shifting within the spectrum of traits that make up their personality type.

It can help significantly in our understanding of others to assess whether someone is in their healthy, average or unhealthy level of functioning.

The nine levels of development are comprised of three levels in the healthy segment, three levels in the average segment and three levels in the unhealthy segment. Shades of grey abound.

The continuum of the levels of development is as follows:

Healthy

Level 1: The level of liberation

Level 2: The level of psychological capacity

Level 3: The level of social value

Average

Level 4: The level of imbalance/social role

Level 5: The level of interpersonal control

Level 6: The level of overcompensation

Unhealthy

Level 7: The level of violation

Level 8: The level of obsession and compulsion

Level 9: The level of pathological destructiveness

Try and be as honest as you can when it comes to assessing your own level. Even though this can sometimes expose uncomfortable truths, it is the surest path to personal growth.

Levels can be understood in terms of our capacity to be present. The further we move down the levels, the less present we are and the more we are identified with the ego and its negative patterns. The lower down the levels we go, the more defensive, compulsive and destructive we become. We tend to be less free, less self-aware, and act on a more sub-conscious level.

Conversely, as we move up the levels, we become more and more present. We are less destructive and increasingly free and open. We are far more self-aware and astute. We are less likely to get caught up in negativity.

Becoming more present allows us to be more objective about our personality and we become adept at self-observation. This makes us more effective in all areas of our lives, whether that be relationships or our career. It can bring genuine peace and joy to whatever it is that we are doing.

Chapter 4: Humans, A Never-Ending Story

As someone who personally has an intense interest in the spiritual—if only as an observer of it—I try to often find new ways to categorize myself and others. It's a part of what makes me, and everyone else, human. People have an instinctual urge to put different kinds of people in different boxes, chalk up different motivations and personality types into just that, types. Charts and graphs that help us get a better, more concrete picture of the people we see every day, including our own reflection. So, it's no surprise that the enneagram test strikes many people, myself included, as a perfect method of visualizing the personality.

There are 9 base "personalities" within the enneagram test, but there are also many add-ons to those basic types. These many different combinations of aspects of the personality allow for the enneagram test to be particularly personalized. Much like a fairly similar personality test, the Myers-Briggs personality examination, the enneagram doesn't rely on a small set of broad descriptions to capture its audience. Instead, it allows for the results of the test from any one person to be much more fluid and flexible, accommodating both the quirks and tendencies of a person on any given day which might deviate from their "normal" personality, and to the relationships and interactions that someone may have any day, which could alter the way they behave drastically.

All of these ways that the enneagram can shift to fit the tendencies of anyone taking the test allow for the experience as a whole to feel much more personalized, as though the singular person taking it feels as though the test is addressing them more personally. Compare this style of test to the zodiac. While many people feel their horoscope was seemingly written "just for them" on any given day, the reality is that many horoscopes are simply littered with blanket statements, sentiments that are so nearly universal that a person can feel as though the horoscope was personalized without it seeming overly obscure. On the other hand, the enneagram has enough add-ons to the basic set of types that depending on how a person takes the test, a set of people who all have the same basic temperament may actually get different answers. It's these many additions to the test that make it more unique, and which make the results of that test much more meaningful.

Of course, we find ourselves often so drawn to the same kinds of personality tests, mostly for the same reasons—we want to know more about ourselves. We sometimes find ourselves relying on other people or tests to tell us things we may have already known about ourselves, if only to hear a second opinion and feel more assured in the fact of the matter. This also allows for sources like the newspaper's horoscope to let loose a barrage of blanket statements without the people reading them really feeling as though the sentiment is too vague for them to relate to. They want to validate and verify things they suspect about themselves. While it would be easy for us to think things of ourselves and make assumptions based on our own behavior, we will never truly have an objective view of ourselves. We'll always be at least slightly biased toward ourselves, whether negatively or positively. Therefore, we look to third parties to educate us about the subject with which we should feel the most familiar. This, of course, leads many people to be drawn into personality tests, the enneagram included. Where the enneagram is different from the rest lies in both its complexity, and its spirituality.

The enneagram is perhaps a bit different from other kinds of personality assessments because it deals in the matter of the soul. Those who follow a more spiritually-driven lifestyle often find much more comfort in this kind of exam as compared to other kinds of tests. The horoscope, however, also finds much of its allure in the spiritual. For example, many people who follow wicca beliefs or participate in them deal with the energy of celestial bodies and the souls. Even to someone who doesn't much believe in the existence of souls at all, even in living things, the idea of some unknown but positive force which connects all life to each other can be very comforting.

Enneagram tests vary slightly depending on who is giving them, or through what outlet they're being given, but most all of them have questions which mostly deal with the soul and the conscience. The enneagram is more of a moral examination, in a way. It doesn't set up types of people in a way that makes one seem better than the other. Rather, the enneagram test is usually more inclined to set up scenarios in which different people act differently according to their specific moral compasses, and proceeds to categorize them by those compasses. While that morality is not entirely genetic, and is always somewhat inherited from the environment that an individual grows up in, there is also always the tendency for a person to deviate from what they're taught by their childhood, especially in more western countries. In a place where culture is shrouded in the ideals of independence and trail-blazing, many people grow up into much different adults than they were as children. Thus, the moral compass is also bound to change based on the experience that people have as a human.

This human experience is what binds us all broadly together, while also separating us, dictates the enneagram. While we are all individuals, it's the camaraderie of our time period, and the struggles that we all go through, which ties us together and breeds empathy. This empathy being one of the major focal points of the different enneagram personality types. For example, one of the basic enneagram types is the fourth type, also known as the individualist type. As the name suggests, the fourth type is much more prone to keep to themselves and tends to prioritize time alone as opposed to time in a group. The ninth type, however, the peacemaker, prides themselves on being able to deescalate situations and is more than willing to compromise for the good of a group. While the priorities of the fourth and the ninth type are often very different, they are both connected by their desire to care for humans, whether that human be first and foremost themselves, or their friends and colleagues. There are many ways like this where some of the enneagram types seem to clash. In reality, though, there is a hidden bond between all of the types, just as many see a hidden bond between all people. It's the strong conviction of many that humans are bound together, and it's scientific fact that humans are predominantly social animals. They need interaction and care from others if they want to survive for long periods of time. So, doesn't it make sense that all different kinds of people are also bound together, no matter what their initial differences?

It's in this book where we explore the human frame of mind and what drives all of the different types to their behavior. Just like every kind of personality test, however, not all results will be the same and not every aspect of your personal type may apply to you. This is the fluidity of the enneagram test—there are some parts which will apply some days, and which couldn't be any farther from the truth on the next day. Because we are human, we are going to change as we go through our life. As such, the type you get when you read the first time will likely not be the type you have for the rest of your life. Often, when people take a test like the enneagram so much as six months or a year apart, the results may differ. We change rapidly as people, and so the results we get from any kind of test will never be quite the same, just as we are never quite the same.

Additionally, the enneagram test is not a test who defines who you are and how you should live your life from here on out, until the end of time. The results you get from the enneagram test are nothing more than a basic guideline into how you likely tend to act in certain scenarios, the ideals you likely have. From these results, you shouldn't feel pressured to draw anything except a guideline, and some advice. All the results give you is a bit of insight into your character, and some of the description may not quite fit your personally. So, be cautious in how you address the information given to you from the test. If you don't like the description of the type you got, it only means that you now have a goal to work toward in changing yourself for the better.

It's not only yourself which should be changed for the better when seeing your final results of the enneagram. This book also serves to educate you on exactly how the enneagram functions to build up your relationships with others. This could be with your friends, your family, new colleagues or a boss, or your significant other. Regardless of who is being helped indirectly through your results, this test will give you an idea of, depending on what type you receive, what is likely faulty, or at risk of becoming faulty, in your relationships with others. It can serve as advice or as a warning, or simply, again, and a general idea of how things are probably going in your relationship, what to focus on and what to watch out for.

All of this being said, it's imperative that you understand the fluidity of this test, its results, and what those results mean. The results can change, and they don't define you. Take that to heart moving forward, as you learn more about the enneagram, and—hopefully—more about yourself.

Chapter 5: The History Of Enneagram

As the old saying goes, everything that has a beginning has an end - and vise versa. Every process has a starting point, and every piece of history is felt in the future. This same situation extends to Enneagram. To fully understand what the term Enneagram means, we would have to go deep into its historical background and development. How did Enneagram begin? What led to its development? How was the idea of Enneagram conceived? There is only one way to find out as this is what this chapter will delve into.

The word Enneagram is from two Greek words, ennea, which means "nine" and gramma meaning "written." The origin of Enneagram has been a notable controversy among scholars. The need arose because many people have found the personalities identified as being true to form even in their personal experiences. One of the earliest writings on the Enneagram, as opined by Palmer and Wiltse is found in the book of Evagrius Ponticus in the 4th century. In his book, Ponticus gave eight personalities, which he called logismoi meaning "deadly thoughts" with the critical thought as "love of self." This was created because Ponticus thought that whatever one does as a judgment of another person's trait is influenced by the personality of that person.

In other words, people with the 'challenger' personality will mostly take 'enthusiasm' as a negative trait simply because they don't exhibit it. To bolster this, Ponticus further says that;

"The first thought of all is that love of self (Philautia); after this [come] the eight."

These identifications given by Ponticus caused a lot of commotion as people wondered how true it was to equate love to personalities. How could love originate without being altered too? In response to that, Ponticus gave the "remedies" to the eight thoughts. These solutions will be used to answer whatever questions that have to do with or would erupt on the ideas. With these remedies, many people saw the need to adopt the thoughts of Ponticus with all carefulness. Whether the resources given to the eight thoughts are still relevant in today's world is debatable.

The eight thoughts didn't, however, get enough publicity. But with the works of G.I. Gurdjieff, the Enneagram was known everywhere. This could have been the origin of what Enneagram is, alongside its study today. It is pertinent to note that Gurdjieff still retained the eight thoughts from Ponticus. As a matter of fact, they served as the guiding tenets of his work.

In modern day, Oscar Ichazo, a Bolivian, could be said to be Enneagram originator. The nine personality studies in this contemporary age are from his lectures, most importantly, those that focus on ego-fixations, virtues, passions, and holy ideas, delivered by Oscar in the 1950s. Another report claims that Oscar's well-detailed self-development and orientation were actually how he started the teaching that begot Enneagram. The lessons on 'Proto-analysis' uses the typical nine enneagram figures and ideas that are used today.

With the growth in awareness of Enneagram through Oscar's teaching, Africa institute based in Chile was established. However, it later moved to the United States of America when he relocated to South America. This is where the etymology of "Enneagram of Personality" can be traced to. Oscar later coined the term. As the enneagram personalities got enough establishments, Oscar needed to teach some of his students so that they would be able to take enneagram personalities around the globe and obviously to the next level.

In the 1970s, notable psychologists such as John Lilly and Claudio Naranjo went to Oscar to learn about the concept of

Enneagram. Little wonder why these two were part of the earliest students of Oscar to understand Enneagram of personality. The Chilean and psychiatrist, Claudio Naranjo (from Arica in Chile) was in Africa Institute to take a course. Naranjo, having learned a great deal from Oscar, decided to start his teachings on Enneagram in the United States.

He took the teaching with a differing view from what his teacher, Oscar, taught him. He influenced some priest, the Jesuit, who adopted it to spiritual dealings. Enneagram took another approach against what Oscar wanted. His different approach, though friendly and straightforward, was perceived by Oscar as shrewd and misunderstanding. Because of this, Oscar disowned Naranjo and labeled his teachings as treacherous even though his lessons with other teachers spread like wildfire in the 1970s. Because Naranjo was teaching his understanding of Enneagram, his theory grew very fast and had students too.

As the saying goes, 'you shall reap what you sow,' Naranjo also witnessed the same thing he did to his teacher as his students also misconstrued and betrayed him in the end. Naranjo taught different things which were taken for spiritual dealings, and his students taught things that seemed to be more business inclined. Instead of preaching their teacher's teachings, they focus on a paradigm shift which saw them exploring the business side of Enneagram.

In the 1980s and 1990s, diverse authors such as Helen Palmer, Richard Rohr, Elizabeth Wagele and Don Richard Riso, started various publications on Enneagram. Meanwhile, the theories they taught and published are a mixture of how Enneagram erupted. In today's enneagram theories, attention to what the context of their application is, solely determined their usage and understanding. As part of the publishers, this book takes no particular view other than simplifying everything concerning Enneagram.

Maybe because enneagram founders understood and taught Enneagram at a different situation, many of Enneagram theories are basically on spirituality and business —as noted in the introduction. In fact, today, many authors would love to equate Enneagram to spirituality. This is very wrong, considering the history of the Enneagram. The account given here was confirmed from different authors and looking at it from different opinions. Enneagram is used in psychology and even neuroscience today. A lot of attention has been drawn to it because of how people have known about it lately.

Be that as it may, it is essential to know that the historical background of Enneagram follows an intricate pattern. From one scholar to another, from one philosopher to another, and from one teacher to another, the Enneagram concept had followed a fantastic design which had led to its rapid development over the past century. Additionally, the idea is still being transformed and developed with new ideas coming from young minds. Now, our next chapter will focus on where the concept of Enneagram was developed.

Chapter 6: Building Self-Understanding

"Who am I?" This is an age-old question—yet how many people have been able to answer this question for themselves with honesty? This chapter is where we get into more of the psychology aspect of learning about personalities. The dictionary defines self-understanding as "awareness of and ability to understand one's own actions and reactions." I'm sure many people wonder how important it is to know themselves. We have so many labels and titles—athlete, mother, singer, married, single. Why would we need to know anything else? If we feel like we get along fine in our everyday lives, then who cares, right? Why delve into the more uncomfortable, emotional aspect of who we are?

So why is self-understanding critical? Knowing ourselves gives us the ability to see our individuality. We don't just blend into the people around us when we understand how we think, how we feel, and what makes us angry or sad. We learn where our weaknesses are and learn to adapt and accept the inevitable changes of an ever-moving world. Self-understanding shows us what we know and what we still need to discover. Hence, oftentimes, we try to hide our weaknesses, which can cause them to appear more prominently to others.

Thus, to understand ourselves better, let's take a look at what "self" is, according to some popular psychological theories.

What is "Self"?

"Self" is a concept with many aspects. We have the physical aspect: how active we are, what we like to do in our spare time, our favorite sports, or hobbies. The social aspect: how we relate to other people, whether we like to hang out in large groups or spend time with a select few or even alone, how deeply we get to know people. The competent aspect: how able we are to take care of ourselves, keep a job, pay rent, whether we take care of ourselves or have families to care for, our ability to complete tasks.

Other primary factors of self are self-knowledge, self-perception, self-esteem, and self-awareness.

Self-Knowledge

The process of gathering self-knowledge is based on a question of its own: "what am I like?" It is not just what we know about ourselves but also our need to seek out knowledge that leads us to a greater understanding of our concept of self. It is a mental representation of who we are as individuals. Individuality is made up of many attributes that we relate to ourselves as we discover the ones that apply. Self-knowledge is found in the realm of cognitive self; the things we both know about ourselves and the things we might think we know. This includes the very physical individual traits, such as ethnicity, eye or hair color, and body build as well as more psychological traits like morals and beliefs.

Self-Perception

Perception is defined as "a way of regarding, understanding, or interpreting; a mental impression." Daryl Bem, a psychologist, has theorized self-perception as it regards to the development of attitudes. Bem claims that people naturally develop attitudes as emotional responses to either ambiguous or previously un-experienced circumstances. We do this by being aware of our behavior and acting accordingly to respond to a situation. This theory has been seen as contradictory; however, many believe it is not our behavior that dictates our attitude but our attitudes themselves that influence behavior. The healthy way to approach self-perception is to examine the possibility that it could go both ways. The fact remains, if we consider the last part of the definition of perception, it comes down to one thing: understanding. If self-knowledge is gathering information about ourselves, then self-perception is the ability to understand that information. We can then understand why we respond and react to different things the way we do.

Self-Esteem

Self-esteem understands on a more personal level. It hits on the longing aspect of our personalities. It is how we see ourselves; our evaluation of our worth, whether it's how other people see us or not. Self-esteem is entirely emotional and can, obviously be positive or negative. Some personalities can not only see themselves as competent, wanted, worthy, or valued; they can believe it as well. Other personalities will yearn to feel all of those beliefs and hear them affirmed by other people but will be unable to accept them or even perceive them for themselves. Unfortunately, it seems much more common for us to believe the negative about ourselves. Many who suffer from low self-esteem see themselves as unworthy, unattractive, or incompetent. Self-esteem plays a vital role in how we operate in our daily lives. It can influence the outcomes of our jobs, how we deal with families and other relationships, even the results of academic pursuits.

Self-Awareness

Self-awareness is the ability to understand that we are our own individuals, apart from everyone else. It is how we can be conscious in the knowledge of our character and personalities, including our emotions, what motivates us, and our likes and dislikes. Self-awareness can be split into two factions: external and internal. External awareness is, naturally, being aware of our own physical body in regards to health, human development, and external interpretation to internal sensations. For this book, we are primarily interested in inner awareness, which is our emotional responses. Part of understanding ourselves is being aware of the emotions we are feeling and what causes those emotions to occur.

Jungian Self Archetype

Carl Jung has produced many helpful theories on self and personalities. The famous Myers-Briggs personality-typing test is based on Jung's theories on introverted and extroverted personalities. Jung believed that there were two levels of our unconscious mind: personal and collective. Evolution plays a big role in this theory and states that there is a "collective" instinctual thought and process pattern that has developed in all of us through centuries of development. He categorized these ancient behaviors into "archetypes." To him, they represented the basis for all social practices, no matter when/where/to whom you were born. A rich man in the city would have the same innate behaviors as an Ecuadorian native living in a hut in the jungle. There is a more comprehensive list of twelve archetypes Jung identified, and they are derived from four main one: Shadow, Anima and Animus, Persona, and Self. The Jungian theory says that Self is the center of the entire personality—including the unconscious, the conscious, and the ego. It is usually symbolized by a circle, as it represents the whole psyche. He claims that Self is not only the most critical archetype—it can be tough to understand. He believed it to be a separate entity, the source of our dreams—and he felt that complete knowledge of true Self was impossible. His theory posed that in the first "phase" of our lives, we are born into the collective "primal" consciousness. As we age, we come into our own personalities—our own "self." His process is involved and a little confusing. It's more psychology than we need for our purposes, but the one thing remains: the self is essential, and learning who we are is the beginning to self-understanding.

Johari Window

Another technique for discovering our self is called the Johari Window. It was developed by two different psychologists: Harrington Ingram and Joseph Luft. The Johari Window gives us four basic versions of the Self: hidden, known, unknown, and blind.

Our hidden self is what we know and perceive in ourselves that is not seen that other people do not. This is where we hide things about ourselves that we don't want to be known. It is very private and protected for a variety of reasons. These are the things we may feel guilty or ashamed of, or we may be too insecure about showing vulnerability. The hidden self could also indicate good qualities of humility and modesty.

Conversely, the known self is naturally the side of us that is known to the world. It is both what we see and what those around us see. We can share our known self to others freely, and we are reconciled to what we and others have defined this side of us to be.

The unknown self is a bit more ambiguous. It is the side of us that neither the world nor we can see. It could mean both negative and positive things that we are not aware of yet. It can also indicate unknown skills or potential; things we just haven't discovered about ourselves yet. Getting to know the hidden self can be intimidating. It means venturing outside of comfort zones, embracing change, and trying new things.

And finally, there is the blind self. This is the area of ourselves that is hidden to us but known by those around us. It also shows misconceptions we may have about who we perceive ourselves to be. Some may think they are focused and organized, while others may disagree. Or we may get hung up on feeling like we are incapable or lack specific skills while others may have an entirely opposite perception. One of the best ways to gain self-understanding and awareness is to get feedback from the people in our lives. It means having the courage to hear both the good and the bad about ourselves, but it is an excellent exercise to consider.

Self-Understanding and the Enneagram

So, now that we have some insight into what "self" is it is time to look into how the Enneagram model can help in our quest for self-understanding. The first step is easy: take the Enneagram test and discover your type. The next step may be more difficult: keep an open mind and accept the bad with the good.

One of the biggest hindrances to gaining this kind of in-depth knowledge is fear. Fear is what keeps us in our boxes: fear of failure, fear of not measuring up, fear of rejection; the list could probably go on for a while. Misuse of the Enneagram tool can lead to more fear and resentment than it is intended to, but a healthy approach to self-evaluation can yield great results.

We should all strive to be better than we are, and that is one of the most important reasons to even attempt to develop a greater self-understanding. That is the whole purpose of the Enneagram model. Even though there are negative sides to every personality, the Enneagram also shows how each personality shines and excels. Before taking the Enneagram test, however, it could be helpful to ask a few pointed questions of ourselves. Questions like: what three words would I use to describe myself? What do I perceive as my top two or three most significant strengths? How would I define my weaknesses? Is there anything I would want to change about myself? Answering these questions as honestly as possible could make identifying with an Enneagram type a bit easier.

We all have gifts and potential; we all have something to offer in any aspect of our lives. We should not see any of the nine personalities as good or bad. They all have good qualities, and they all have blind spots. The Enneagram already identifies the main potential blind spots in each type. Once we have defined our core personality, part of self-understanding is accepting the blind spots and improving on them.

Chapter Conclusion

There are so many outside factors leading to our understanding of self. We are significantly influenced by the when and where we are born, who our parents are, how we are raised, and the environment where we grow up. The good thing is: it doesn't have to end there. That's part of what makes the Enneagram model so helpful. Understanding what motivates our thoughts and actions can help break debilitating thoughts and habits.

Chapter 7: The Enneagram

Everyone is unique. We each have different likes and dislikes, with different tendencies to respond to others. Two people exposed to the same situation will respond in entirely different manners, thanks to the differences in personality. Personalities are endlessly fascinating to people as we try to understand the personality types of other people. Look at the Myers-Briggs Personality Test or the way someone will casually mention being a Type A person. Despite how endlessly unique people are, we like to put everything into neat little categories and boxes that are easy to understand. This is exactly what the Enneagram does: It places people into categories in order to develop a more thorough understanding of those particular people.

Personalities

Before making a point to delve into the Enneagram, let's first take a look at what makes us who we are—personalities. When talking about your personality, you are discussing several characteristics that come together to create you. They identify the differences in characteristics—for example, one person may be optimistic while the other is pessimistic to a fault. This is a personality difference. Some people are even-tempered, while others are hot-headed. Some are introverted, while others are extroverted. There are several personality traits that could be discussed, typically coming in opposing pairs, and we as people are made up of several of these personality traits, all coming together in unique ways to create us.

These personality types dictate our gut reactions—our natural tendency will be to act according to our personality types. If you are typically hot-headed, for example, you are more inclined to explode at even the most minute of inconveniences, such as getting stuck at a red light, but if you have a tendency toward being patient, you may be more inclined to roll with the flow and not care as much. Of course, that does not mean that the patient person will never lose her temper or that the person with a temper is never going to address a problem calmly, but their general predisposition will be to respond in those ways.

There has been much debate over whether personality type is a product of nature or nurture. When discussing the nature vs. nurture debate, nature refers to whether something is inherent to that individual, such as something that is controlled by genetics. When something is said to be a product of nature, people are born with that particular trait without any external factors having an influence. Something controlled by nurture, on the other hand, is influenced by the environment. When thinking about nurture, think of the idea that a child raised in a healthy, loving home would then grow up to be healthy and loving as well while a child who grew up in an abusive home would likely go on to continue the cycle of abuse in the future.

In reality, the cause of personality is somewhere in the middle. In part, it is inherited. We inherit the traits of our parents via genetics. However, those traits only provide the foundation. They provide the possibilities of what could be if given the right environment. Nurture then provides the influence needed to activate specific traits. This is why someone who has grown up in, for example, an abusive household is likely to have very specific personality traits, such as being defensive, lacking trust toward others, or possibly a people-pleaser in an attempt to avoid future abuse.

Personality is an accumulation of several aspects: It is a combination of character and behavior. Now, that may sound simple enough, but let's break that down. Character itself is already an amalgamation of both temperament and learned tendencies. Temperament is the genetic component—it is what you are genetically predisposed toward, while learned habits may sway that toward tendencies that are more socially or culturally acceptable. Behavior then is the way that the individual is actually acting. When you take these three concepts, temperament, learned tendencies, and behavior and combine them, you create personality.

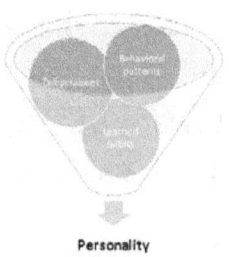

Personality

Personality is the grand total. It is the end result of combining current or potential behavioral patterns that have been determined through genetics and the environment, and it controls nearly every aspect of your life. Your personality is largely stable throughout your life, and it will directly influence your natural reactions to everything. This is why understanding your true personality is so important. When you understand yourself, you will be able to use your personality to your advantage, ensuring that you are always behaving exactly how will benefit you the most.

What Is the Enneagram?

This is where the Enneagram comes in. The Enneagram can be understood simply by looking at its etymology:

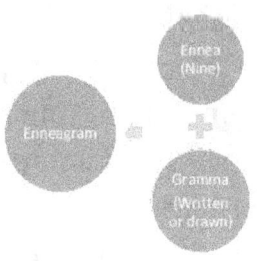

Its roots come from the Greek words for nine and written, which is quite accurate—the Enneagram is represented by an image of a circle with a triangle within it and nine points along the circumference, connecting to other points, each corresponding with a specific personality type. It is a model of understanding that these personality types are interconnected. The figure itself is an enneagram, while the personality types are Enneagrams types.

The nine types of personalities each provide an ego fixation, a holy idea, a passion, and a virtue. Together, along with a general explanation of the individual type's most commonly known traits, you are able to understand the tendencies of someone with that personality type. This is what makes quite useful—if you know for a fact what someone's Enneagram type is, you can tell plenty of information about them, ranging from their motivators to their tendencies under stress. Of course, you should make it a point not to stereotype—just because a Type One Perfectionist got annoyed because something came out subpar does not mean that you can necessarily completely disregard their opinions or feelings as being typical and, therefore, irrelevant.

As you read, keep in mind that, depending on the author or teacher that you are following in regards to the Enneagram, you may encounter different names for the same exact Type. Some of the alternative names for the Types will be included when you are reading about each of the Types in their own chapter, but the names used in this book will be:

The Perfectionist

The Helper

The Performer

The Romantic

The Observer

The Loyal Skeptic

The Epicure

The Protector

The Mediator

These Types will be the primary motivator for the behaviors of an individual. They will dictate the most common tendencies that the individuals will exhibit, as well as predict their most likely responses to stress or relaxation. When you look at the type, you are acknowledging the primary type someone is.

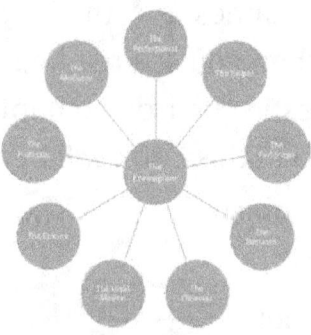

Beyond just the primary types, there are also wings and connecting lines to keep in mind as well in order to get the most out of understanding the Enneagram. Each of these serves primary purposes that should not go neglected or ignored.

Wings

Most theorists of the Enneagram believe that the primary personality type is modified based on those types surrounding it on the enneagram figure. These adjacent types are commonly referred to as wings. If you were to refer to the chart of the types above and choose one point on it, such as The Romantic, the surrounding two Types, in this case, The Performer and The Observer would be the wings. These lend credence to the idea that the Enneagram itself exists on a spectrum rather than nine distinct points, which is important to remember—the Enneagram Type someone has is the one that they most closely relate to, but they do not have to encompass all personality points or tendencies, and they may draw tendencies from either wing as well as well.

Connecting Lines

The connecting lines that go between points add further information to glean about personalities. These lines are often referred to as the security and stress points and are important to keep in mind as well. The Romantic, a Type 4 individual, for example, has a stress point of Type 2 and a security point of Type 1. This means that, in times of stress, the Type 4 individual is likely to take on some traits of a Type 2 individual, while shifting into the Type 1 personality when relaxed. This means, then, that beyond the primary personality type, an individual has their two wings and their two connecting lines that all interact together to create the tendencies that they are likely to exhibit.

The History of the Enneagram

The history of the Enneagram is largely up for debate—it had existed for so long in some form that it is not entirely known when the first instance was. It has been suggested that the work of Evagrius Ponticus, a mystic who lived in Alexandria in the 4th century, came up with similar ideas to the Enneagram—in particular, he created eight deadly thoughts with one more thought known as the love of self. These deadly thoughts had remedies. With the pattern of nine, it is believed by some to be the earliest historical reference to the Enneagram.

However, the individual recognized as the creator of the nine personality types is believed to be a Bolivian man—Óscar Ichazo in the 1950s. He focused his attention on self-development, which he referred to as protoanalysis, utilizing the enneagram figure within it. Using his ideas, he founded the Arica Institute in Chile, before eventually moving to the United States. He is responsible for the term "Enneagram of Personality."

It did not end there—Claudio Naranjo, a Chilean-born psychiatrist, discovered the Enneagram of Personality when taking a course in Arica. He then focused on understanding this process as well, seeking to better understand and influence the Enneagram. In the 1970s, he began teaching his own understanding, which was brought to priests who began to adopt the Enneagram to fit their own spirituality.

Ichazo did not approve of this use of his material, however, and he disowned Naranjo and any teachers underneath him due to feeling like his own beliefs and information was being misinterpreted. The misinterpretation was critical enough for him to entirely disown it all. However, Naranjo was not the only individual who began to differ in their assertions and beliefs surrounding the Enneagram. Several other authors began to publish books that became popular—Don Richard Riso, Richard Rohr, Helen Palmer, and more all began to assert their own beliefs. This is why you start to see differing names for each of the personality types—they were tweaked over time as they became what they are today.

Of all of these people, however, it was someone entirely unrelated who brought Enneagram to common knowledge—George Gurdjieff, an Armenian philosopher, mystic, and spiritual teacher, brought what is commonly referred to as Fourth Way Enneagram into existence. The difference here was that the Fourth Way enneagram includes musical notes depicted as do re mi fa sol la si at points around the circle, with 3 and 6 remaining blank as shock points.

Chapter 8: How Can You Figure Out What Kind Of Personality You Are?

The Enneagram is an unbelievable character writing instrument utilized by others and teachers interested in near home and otherworldly improvement. From the Enneagram, you will find nine varied personality types and three concentrates - or bands of three - of comprehensions, such as heart disease and gut. Additionally, in each group of three, you will find 3 varied personality types.

The centre set of 3 untruth types 3, 2, and 4. Type two is the Giver, 3 is the Performer, and 4 is the Romantic (similarly occasionally called "Sad Romantic"). All vibe at home in their sense focus or the centre focus.

All these Three kinds possess a fervent thermometer that's heading out to the world and analysing everyone it catches. They come to an area, and it is almost like they could test the people inside the room. They are experiencing concerns such as, "Are they feeling? How are they reacting to me? What is their sincerely content?"

Types 3, 2, and 4 - it is about Picture

Types 3, 2, and 4 will be the core tern ion and, therefore, are feeling located. They feel totally comfy, linking with the world through the atmosphere, and they're focused around the image - on how they're seen.

They Aren't only in accord with your responses or ardent substance; they are similarly continually altering themselves because they're concerned about the way you're responding to them. They're constantly shifting themselves to what view to be the passionate responses. Each of those three kinds seems varied when they get it done.

Types 3, 2, and 4 have a simple conviction that they need to win admiration or a sense of worth. Their interior feeling of self would be, to a fantastic extent, subject to what's reflected back to them. Exactly what the outside world discovers in these goes toward getting exactly what their identity is. This is where their thought is normally attracted - towards other people' ardent reaction to them. They're based around what they say and do - the way they expect and maintain themselves. It is about looks.

Also, this "photograph thing" continues endlessly. It's reflected in the energy they set out, the way they walk, and the way they precede. It is even from the terminology that they use; for example, you can view Sort 3 (Achiever) obtaining the speech in a given collecting or social preference.

Sort 4 is connected with whatever someone may say that will make them feel not precisely - or outwardly - the amassing. Genuinely they've this colossal reactivity for this and response to it.

Also, Type 2's are focusing on each of the feelings each other individual is having, and what's happening. They are asking, "How can I help out you without a doubt about it?" It's completely tuned all into sense; that's why it is referred to as the Picture Point - they're creating their image determined by the ardent way others react to them.

Underneath The exterior of 2's, 3's, and 4's, there's bitterness and disgrace. As they begin doing their job, they will, for the most part, opportunity upon concealed signs of the disgrace of exactly what their identity is, and see they have reimbursed by hard as yet another individual.

Their Contemplations are operating across the lines of, "There's something down there which is not directly within me. I cannot give people access too close because that internal imperfection might be found. They could come in, nevertheless not quite near. They might discover that thing."

Types 5, 6 and 7 - the Emotional Triad

Types 5, 6, and 7 would be the head-based types, using underlining of fear and anxiety.

They Reside in the world of justification, insight, and strategizing. The movement they have made into the mind is tied in with creating control and wellbeing where they will not be "down at the chaotic feelings" in which they're rampant and communication using "different things" out on Earth.

Their Concerns go something like, "Up in mind, I will try to receive it. I will completely consider matters. I am able to make a version for how this planet works, and following I push my version on the Earth, and I start to take the version much progressively afterward, I take that the entire world."

The Mental types are strategized - often adroit players. They understand the world and societal circumstances throughout the head marginally then through the centre (feelings) are the body (intestine). They're working on the eyes. They're seeing and visiting to react to speeches, as an instance, "How are people responding - at a reasoning fashion - to me personally "And "What is happening here?"

All of the mind types, there's normally a basic matter of earth. For the 5, people come too close, and there's an institution. From this, query generates, and they escape from the world for a part of their process.

Sort 6's is moving out and in. Nevertheless, their query is out there around Earth. They imagine, "I cannot trust the market." Nonetheless, it's additionally an inward sense, and they are also figuring, "I cannot confide in me." Hence there's a good deal of polarity within the sixes.

The 7 is a larger volume of an externalized trust. Their focal point of thought is outside on Earth, some of their time consuming away their position yet also not feeling good with this. Now the feelings of fear as well as the nerves may show out on Earth, significantly progressively afterward they could indoors.

Types 8, 9 and 1 - at the Human Body and Gut

Types 8, 9, and 9 will be the human body (or intestine) - based types. They feel things throughout the body. They make lively hits. If they stroll to space, it is not about the feeling or believing; instead, they are presuming, "How can this person feel to me down in my gut?"

The body kinds, there's hidden displeasure or even disdain that often appears as ruling. For Type 9, if outrage becomes subdued, they do not really let it outside. What is more, their demands become subdued.

The off probability that you converse with a "young 9" just beginning to perform their own job, they will likely answer, "Outrage, exactly what exactly are you talking? I am definitely the most eloquent, giddy, calm individual, I understand. I really don't know outrage.

Be that as it might, as they proceed farther into themselves, which outrage winds up apparent and is frequently a doorway for them. They'll come across an unheard-of degree of mindfulness and articulation. With no precedent for their own lives, they will understand what their needs are and exactly what they require.

Sort 8 will generally externalize that the outrage. Their energy is a good deal greater, and it ends up. It may overpower people, and outrage can flood into the entire world. They likewise tend not to have a sense of other's limitations. They obtain their displeasure outside and enjoy facing others in a similar manner.

Sort 1 turns the bitterness internal. They will describe an inward pundit - a making a determination about gender - which is riding them. It is normally saying something like, "You have to do it along those lines. This is what you fouled up. You're moronic. You are not doing so right. You are not filled with sense. You aren't aroused enough. You're not (anything) enough.

This Displeasure is concealed, nevertheless regularly, they could similarly be awfully judgmental and lots of distinct individuals. There's an insubordinate inside section for them. Type 1 will generally clutch the displeasure within their bodies.

So, these are the three "Focuses of Intelligence" - the centre (Types 2, 3 and 4 using a hidden difficulty or disgrace), the mind (types 5, 6 and 7 using a basic dread or uneasiness), along with the entire body (types 8, 9 and 1 having fundamental bitterness or judgment).

Self-learning Can be engaging, along with the Enneagram, which is meant to assist you in showing some crucial portions of yourself that might not be quickly self-evident. It may inform you regarding your trends -- exactly what you are most likely going to select when given different choices. Additionally, it informs you regarding your deeper life goals, your needs and especially the qualities. Your qualities encourage what you require a stab at, and will allow you to clarify your objectives.

It does not be that as it might, inform you concerning the type of aptitudes which you have and just how well you have learned them. Neither does it have a great deal to say about your abilities; for example, no matter whether you are good with numbers or possess excellent spatial abilities.

The Enneagram Can Provide the corresponding benefits throughout your own life and work:

• Fosters mindfulness and significant contemplation

• Permits You to Find out how the World may seem from other points of view

• It lets you form new, positive practices

• It enables one to comprehend and break Free of illustrations

• It motivates you're progressively Caring and understanding with other people

Chapter 9: Enneagram Test

The essence of the Enneagram test is to determine your type. Your Enneagram type may change over time. It's not your underlying type that changes; it's actually how you move around in the world.

You will move around the circumference of the circle; you may move across the lines. So who you are today may be different from one year ago, two years ago, five years ago, ten years ago, in terms of how you show up in the world. At the same time, your knowledge of yourself is always increasing with age. Your awareness of your behavior patterns, your awareness of your thoughts, and your feelings are different today than it was when you were young or younger, and that may cause you to show up as another type.

It's worth going through this exercise with a fresh pair of eyes. I'm going to present to you all the different nine types probably in a way you haven't seen or read about before. I'm going to use a lot of images that are easier and clearer to help you identify your type.

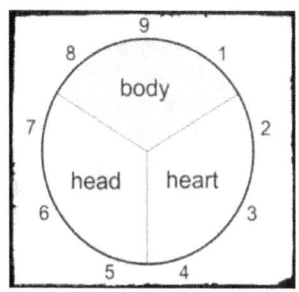

We have three centers in the Enneagram:

Body Center

Heart center and

Head Center

We also have the **Process Enneagram**. They are two different types of Enneagram. We're going to go through each of the nine types, the stress triggers and behaviors that limit their ability to give and receive love.

Due to movements along the lines, the wings, and arrows, you're going to exhibit stress behaviors of all 9 types at some point in your life, and you also may be directly connected to five or six types.

Take enneagram type 1, for example.

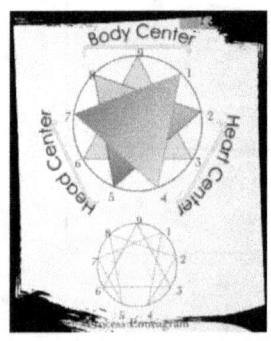

If you look at the diagram, the 1s are connected to 9, which is 1 with a 9 wing, or you can be 1 with a 2 wing.

Each type has two wings on either side. If you compress two of your wings together, you get the main type. Type 1 is kind of a combination of 9 and 2 - you squash them together to get type 1. These two types are very interrelated to each other. 9 and

1 are very close, 1 and 2 are very close. So it's very easy to be positioned around the circumference of the circle whereby you are in a space, you're not sure whether you're 1 wing 2 or 2 wing 1 that's very common.

At the same time, you can move along the line. 1 is also connected to 4 and 7; it's got the 1-4-7 triangle, the idealist triangle.

The process Enneagram shows how you can move under stress or growth. Under stress, 1 would move towards 4; if you are a stressed-out 1, you may show up as 4. If you're 1 who's a bit more relaxed, you may show up as 7, but actually, your core underlying type is a 1. You see, if type 1 is your core type, you could easily show up as a 9,1, 2, 4, or 7. You could show up as five different types quite easily without.

Type 2 is a little bit more complicated in the sense that you're not only connected to 1 and 3 on the original enneagram diagram. You're also connected to 5 and 8.

So you have 1, 2, and 3 as a core part of 2, and you also have 5 and 8. But if you flip across to the process Enneagram, which is how you function in everyday life, a 2 under stress goes to 8 and can also go to 4. So you've got an additional line to 4 if you are type 2.

So if you're type 1, you could be a combination of 5 types, if you are type 2, you could be a combination of 6 types which you can easily show up in stress behaviors of 6 types very easily.

Therein lays one of the biggest challenges and difficulties in using the enneagram because you could easily show up at either of the 6 points, and you may not know which your core point is. But eventually, once you work with the system long enough, you will have to learn how to integrate all five and six different types out of your core type structure to be more balanced and complete as an individual and reduce those stress behaviors which you may manifest.

No one type is better than another; all types have their strengths and weaknesses. There's no point wishing you're another type because if you are a type, you will have to deal with that type's weaknesses and stress behaviors too.

You may be asking, 'why only 9 types?'

Well, naturally, everyone is a unique and wonderful individual, and you are much more than your type, but there are patterns of behavior that exist in human interactions, and these nine types have been confirmed over the years through studies and interviews all over the world for more than forty years. Thousands of interviews have confirmed the existence of these nine types, which is strong scientific and anecdotal evidence that there are nine main types. You're very unique and very different, and how you show up as a type 1 may be different from other 1s and so on, but you will have some things in common.

Chapter 10: Empaths And Relationships

As an empath, navigating relationships in your life can be challenging, especially if you are not actively in tune with your intuition. Empaths have a tendency to find themselves being sucked into unhealthy relationships as a result of their desire to "save" the people around them. This is not so much as an inner desire to be a savior as a symptom of feeling other people's energies as deeply as they do and experiencing deep and intense compassion for them. Even so, empaths can be particularly vulnerable to abusive relationships as a result of this deep inner compassion.

Learning how to navigate your relationships effectively is important if you are going to be engaging in relationships that allow you to thrive as an empath. You need to learn how to identify toxic relationships, how to handle yourself when toxic behaviors arise, and what you can do to ensure that your needs are also being met in your relationships.

Navigating Relationships as an Empath

As an empath, you need to be particularly cautious about the relationship that you enter in your life. Even seemingly harmless relationships such as those that you share with your coworkers or your boss can quickly become toxic if you are not careful. If you have already noticed this toxicity arising in these relationships, you may find yourself struggling to decide how to proceed so that you can avoid being taken advantage of or emotionally or energetically abused. In that case, you need to learn how to navigate your relationships with others.

The first and primary tool that you need to rely on in every single relationship is your intuition. As you know, your intuition is your superpower as an empath, and learning how to behave in alignment with your intuition is imperative if you are going to avoid unwanted experiences. If you find yourself in a relationship that you are questioning, in terms of toxicity, chapter 8 will be extremely helpful for you in navigating these relationships. Otherwise, your intuition will allow you to discover when people are being genuine towards you or when they are breaching your boundaries. Many times, empaths will enter relationships with perfectly healthy people and will accidentally teach those people to ignore their boundaries because they are inexperienced with having and upholding boundaries. As an empath, you are going to need to start intuitively deciding where your boundaries are and feeling into it any time you believe that your boundaries have been breached. That way, you can ensure that you are asserting yourself when you need to and that you are avoiding turning otherwise healthy relationships into toxic ones through your own toxic behaviors.

Troubles That May Arise in Relationships

As an empath, one of the most common troubles that will arise is your tendency to attract narcissists and other energetic vampires into your life. They seem to be able to sense the empathic energies of people and will quickly take advantage of an empath they meet as soon as they meet one, including yourself. If you want to avoid being taken advantage of, you have to be willing to lean into your intuition and genuinely pay attention to the signs of how people are treating you and what it truly means.

The second trouble that commonly arises for empaths is the tendency to become codependent because of how challenging it can be to navigate social situations on their own. You may find yourself clinging to one or two people who you are particularly close to who make you feel comfortable when you are together. In some cases, this may be a healthy friendship or relationship, but in other cases, it may turn into you becoming dependent on this other individual to help you in public experiences. Even if they are a genuine and kind-hearted person, this type of dependency can lead to many troubles for you, so it is ideal to avoid these types of codependent relationships with people.

Your Needs as an Empath

As an empath, you have unique needs in relationships that may be quite different from the needs of those around you. Because you are more sensitive and vulnerable to the energies of those around you, you need to be ready to identify what your needs are and assert them as you move through your relationship. Remember, your needs are going to be quite different from others and the people you enter relationships with may not be empaths themselves, meaning that you are going to have to be ready to stand up for yourself. You will need to ensure that you are in a relationship where you feel confident in standing up for yourself, and where you standing up for yourself are honored by those around you.

Below are the five needs that you must consider before entering a relationship with anyone, or continuing a relationship with anyone if you are an empath.

You Need to Maintain Your Alone Time

As an empath, you are going to need to ensure that you do not fall into the vices of codependency by maintaining your alone time and learning to stay emotionally and energetically sound on your own. It can be easy to find a person that you feel safe around and who "gets" you and want to exclusively spend your time with this person, but falling into this habit can be dangerous. If you are not careful, you may find yourself building up codependency towards others, which can extremely inhibit your own ability to feel complete and whole by yourself.

In addition to you personally choosing to maintain your alone time, you also need to ensure that the other half in your relationships are willing to allow you to enjoy your alone time as well. For some people, the amount of alone time that you need or when it is needed may seem unreasonable or confusing to them. It is important that they understand that even if it does not make sense to them, they still need to respect your need for solitude. They should know that during this time, you will not be available to talk, spend time together, or be around anyone aside from yourself because you need this time to recharge.

If you are in a relationship where this is not yet being honored, make sure that you are honest with this person about your need for alone time and that you make it clear as to why you need it. If they do not understand terms like "empath," simply say that you feel overwhelmed when you are around too much at once and you occasionally need complete solitude to recharge. Sometimes, saying it in a very plain and straightforward way can help it make more sense to other people.

You Need to Be Heard and Respected

In any relationship you enter, you need to be heard and respected in that relationship. This is true for any relationship, but as an empath, you may find it challenging to assert yourself in this way and you might find yourself willingly letting other people ignore you or disrespect your wishes. This is not necessarily due to a lack of self-respect or a lack of desire to be cared for, but because you struggle to assert yourself for fear of what emotional and energetic backlash you might face. It may feel uncomfortable for you to speak up and declare that you do not feel heard or respected, which might mean that instead of asserting yourself, you say nothing and try to "make do" with what happens.

If you are entering a new relationship, pay close attention to how that person listens and how they respect you after you have voiced your needs or concerns. If they listen and they respect you, chances are that they are a positive person to enter a relationship with. If they do not, however, or they respect you for a short period of time and then later disrespect you or say it was "too big of a request" (this is common with narcissists), then you should avoid this relationship. These types of relationships can become emotionally and mentally draining and are especially dangerous to vulnerable empaths.

If you are in a relationship where you feel as though you are not being heard or respected by the other person, you need to speak up for yourself and voice your concerns. Let them know that you are trying to be heard but that you feel as though they are not listening to you, or that they hear you but they are not respecting your wishes. If they change, your problem may have been inside of a communication error that you were struggling with. If they don't, you may be in a relationship with a narcissist or an energy parasite and you need to end that relationship or minimize your exposure to that person as much as possible.

You Need to Stay Open and Honest

Aside from having the other person listen to you more intently and clearly, you also need to be willing to speak up for yourself and do your best to be heard. As an empath, you may feel that you have been taught to stay quiet or say nothing for fear of what energetic or emotional consequences you might face if you told the truth. This is highly common, but it can also be highly destructive to you if you are trying to engage in more positive relationships but keep finding yourself being steamrolled by those in your life.

As you begin to develop new relationships in your life, seek to start off on the foot of being honest and upfront with the person you are entering a relationship with. Rather than getting into the habit of minimizing yourself or shrinking yourself for their benefit, get into the habit of standing strong in your position and being clear and honest in your needs.

For the relationships that you are already in, focus on undoing your habits around staying quiet or not speaking up for yourself and start focusing on being actually heard by the other half in your relationships. This will take some time as you may have already developed unhealthy habits in your relationships, but the more you set the intention of working through them, the sooner you will be able to grow away from these habits.

Your Partner Needs to Be Emotionally Intelligent

As an empath, especially if you are entering a relationship with someone who is not an empath, you should be looking for emotional intelligence in people. People who are emotionally intelligent will generally have a better sense of control over their emotions, which means that they will be less likely to become harmful through their emotions. Rather than blowing up when they are angry, guilt tripping you when they are sad, or being overbearing with their jealousy, they will know how to manage their emotions and refrain from spilling them all over others. As an empath, this means that you can feel more confident around them and their ability to manage their emotions, thus meaning that you are less likely to become harmed through their poor emotional management.

As you enter new relationships, look to see how they handle their emotions in general. Avoid getting blinded by how they are treating you during the earliest stages of your relationship when they are likely trying to make a good impression and look for other clues instead. See what they say about how they have treated others in the past or experiences they have had with other people, and pay attention to how they treat those around you. If you see them spending time around their friends or family, pay close attention to their behavior because these are the relationships where they will act the most authentic to who they really are. If they are not kind, compassionate, or empathetic towards others in their life, chances are they will not be kind, compassionate, or empathetic towards you when you get closer to them. As a result, you can conclude that it may be a poor relationship for you to enter.

If you are in a relationship with someone who is not emotionally intelligent and who tends to spill their emotions everywhere, you are going to need to start asserting verbal and energetic boundaries. With your boundaries, you can start preventing their energy from leaking into your energy field and teach them to stop spilling all of their emotions onto you. While opening up and confiding in you is one thing, taking their emotions out on you or confiding in you if you have expressed that you do not currently have the time or energy to invest in listening is not okay. Assert this boundary and ensure that they respect it, or consider ending your relationship with this person if they don't.

Your Partner Needs to Be Considerate Of Your Needs

Lastly, the second half of your relationship, whether it is with a lover or a coworker, should always be considerate of your needs. If you plan on spending a lot of time around a person and investing energy into building a relationship with them, you need to make sure that they not only respect you but also consider you and your needs. A great example of someone considering your needs would be if you were to confide in someone about your sensitivities and then they asked you how you were feeling during high energy outings that you shared. This proves that not only will they respect your need to manage your energy, but that they will also consider your needs and ask about your feelings. Not everyone is going to show this level of consideration, especially if it is just an acquaintance, but if someone wants to be closer with you, they should express consideration for you and your needs in one way or another.

As you enter new relationships, look for people who show compassion and consideration for your needs as an empath. If they do, chances are that they are a kind of person who is going to think about you and be respectful of you as an empath. If they don't, they may be too self-absorbed for you to comfortably engage with given your unique needs. However, make sure that you are looking out for consideration and not service: you want someone who is considerate towards you, not a servant.

In your current relationships, look for the people who show true consideration towards you and nurture those relationships. In relationships with anyone who may not outwardly express consideration for you and your needs, consider whether or not they respect you and if you feel safe and cared for in your relationship. If you do not, or if you feel like you are consistently ignoring your needs for them, you might want to reconsider your relationship with this person.

Your Quick Start Action Step: Audit Your Relationships

Your quick action step today is to audit your relationships and start paying attention to where you can improve the relationships that you already have in your life. If you need to, start speaking up more and asserting your boundaries in your relationships more so that your loved ones can begin respecting you and your needs. If you have tried this and they continue to ignore you or refuse to change the way they treat you, you might consider ending your relationship with that person. It can be challenging to end relationships, particularly if you have a great deal of compassion and love for the other person, but in some cases, it is completely necessary.

Chapter 11: Ennea-Type Four – "The Individualist"

Aliases: The Tragic-Romantic. The Artist. The Sensitive, Withdrawn Type.

Generally described as:

ExpressiveSelf-Absorbed

DramaticTemperamental

At their best, Type Fours are described as:

InspiredTransformative

ImaginativeNostalgic

Motto: "I am unique. I'm the only person who feels this way, and no one else can really understand."

The Individualist in General

People who exhibit a Core Type Four have a strong desire to feel unique and special, and actively work to distinguish themselves from others. They place a priority on discovering their "true selves" and being "satisfied with life." Type Four people genuinely desire to experience what life has to offer and are concerned about being perceived as individuals.

They often experience intense emotional highs and lows, even to the point of their emotions being expressed in raw, unfiltered form. Individualists long for a life of meaning, which they may see as lying in the past or future. By focusing on their fantasies, they may eventually disconnect from the people in their present.

When a Type Four person can fully engage and express themselves, they inspire and lead others. They will enjoy exploring both the dark and joyful aspects of life, relishing the emotional honesty and their attempts to convey their feelings to others. They make excellent, empathetic listeners who can give friends and loved ones a fresh perspective and insight into creative solutions, as it is natural for them to ask questions, seek reactions, and support others' individual growth.

Sometimes, while a Type Four person works to get to know someone, they are reserved, hesitant to show the vulnerabilities of their true emotions. They greatly fear being ordinary or misunderstood, and being rejected, so they may shut out others until they feel their individuality will be accepted. Individualists prefer to be seen as mysterious, rare, genuine people who will never really be understood.

When a Type Four person develops their identity to the point where they feel secure in expressing it wholeheartedly, they feel fulfilled. With a natural quiet strength, they can objectively evaluate their emotions and behaviors and adjust to align with who they "really are inside." They receive immense pleasure from recognizing uniqueness in others, and praising truth, beauty, and depth of emotion in others' creations.

How Individualists See Themselves vs. How Others See Them

Individualists see themselves as talented and special, set apart from other people. However, this self-appreciation can come across as rude, arrogant, or judgmental. While their attitude tends to isolate them, they crave attention and acceptance, because what good is it to be unique, if no one sees it? They think they are driven by a true desire to stand out – to be one-of-a-kind – but actually, Individualists generally operate from deep fear of being alone. Although the Individualist believes that their individualism is a gift, it also often acts as their own curse.

Individualists are invested in interpersonal relationships. They care about the feedback they receive from others and are sensitive and self-conscious. Although they can feel like social outcasts, or at least, socially awkward, they are also driven by feelings of love and can be incredibly romantic. They long for ideals – of time, of place, and of relationships – and nurture this desire internally while imposing their ideals on the outside world.

Because Type Fours are inclined to view themselves at outsiders, acceptance and generosity may surprise them. It may take an Individualist time to "warm up" to relationships, but once they bond with someone, they can become as invested in that person as themselves. Individualists can be prone to jealousy, which causes them to withdraw from someone they envy. They may criticize others to try to cover their disappointment in themselves. Although unable to express it, they often long to live with the ease and comfort they see in others – free from emotional pressures.

While the Individualist Ennea-type can see themselves as the embodiment of free agency and self-expression, they can come across to others as insensitive, critical, aloof, or petty. The Individualist can see themselves as nurturing the beauty within themselves, but others may see the Individualist as "acting ugly" or "weird."

The "Average" Individualist's Mental Health

When an Individualist is at an average level of health, they may engage actively in the world, then regularly withdraw to an interior world to process events and feelings. They are sensitive and creative, intuitive and imaginative, but can become protective of feelings, fighting to contain them, hiding them from others. Sometimes seen as shy and moody, Individualists can be "aloof" and hypersensitive at the same time.

When an Individualist feels better than average, they may romanticize life and become nostalgic, dreaming of the past or future. At this level, an Individualist wants to create and grow an interesting and beautiful world around themselves, because they feel passions and observations they are driven to express. Although they desperately desire to bloom, they are self-conscious and deeply afraid of others' criticism.

Moving Toward Integration: Individualists At Their Best

When moving in their Direction of Integration (growth) and exhibiting their best qualities, Individualists become calm and objective, able to shed their jealousy and emotional baggage.

Basic Desire(s): To express their genuine creativity and unique perspective; to create a satisfying, authentic identity.

Basic Motivation(s): To feel, create, and express their inner beauty. Driven to be seen as unique, and to attract special attention.

Unique Gift(s): Experience intense emotions, which they attempt to use to connect with others. Imaginative and wild, they work to make the world a better, more beautiful place.

Basic Goal: Become authentic through personal expression.

Honest, objective, and empathetic, Type Four people at their best are not afraid to look at their flaws and reveal their vulnerabilities. They make others comfortable and uplift them with a spirit of whimsy and acceptance. They are open-minded, soft-hearted, and above all truly unlike anyone else. They inspire, motivate, and love wholeheartedly.

When Individualist's Mental Health is Excellent

When at their best, Individualists inspire. They refuel their own creative energy through personal expression, becoming more energized with every creation or idea. Deeply curious, they seek the truth in themselves and spend their energy analyzing and interpreting how they feel about their experiences. Once they find value in the world and can express it, the results transform people.

As Type Four people Disintegrate, they shift their introspective energy to a more self-centered, even rebellious, mindset.

Self-conscious and aware of others' reactions to their emotional expressions, Type Four people become mocking and judgmental, or may sink into melancholy or depression, as they seek to hide their underlying vulnerabilities.

Moving Toward Disintegration: Individualists When Stressed

When moving in their Direction of Disintegration (stress), the normally whimsical and independent Individualist regresses, becoming highly needy or disconnected and aloof.

Basic Fear(s): Afraid of not establishing an authentic identity and value.

Triggering Emotion(s): **Jealousy**

When Fixated: **Melancholy**

What Type Four People Might Struggle With

Type Four people can suffer from depression, self-pity, and anxiety related to frustrated feelings or a sense of disconnect.

Individualists can become self-indulgent and nostalgic, wishing for their fantasies to come true. They can develop an ideal self-image that isn't aligned with the way they act, and they can lie to protect themselves from feeling inadequate or boring. They might spend time and energy convincing others that they are flawed or pitiful, while expecting the other person to try to convince them otherwise.

Type Fours tend to exaggerate, both the pleasurable and the painful, both the darkness and the light. The need to be loved and appreciated can both fuel them to push themselves further and complicate their intense desire not to be judged.

When Individualist's Mental Health is Struggling

When fully disintegrated and under stress, Individualists can feel hopeless, in despair, and trapped under the weight of their experiences and emotions. When unable to genuinely express themselves or losing connections with others, Type Four people wade through feelings of shame, exhaustion, and self-reproach, which can be a dangerous self-perpetuating cycle.

As Individuals decrease their stress and focus on higher levels of health, they become more forgiving and hopeful. Although Type Four people seek independence, they also crave connection, and experiences that result in strong emotional reactions help the Individualist maintain a healthy, positive mindset.

Potential Addictive Struggles

Type Four people might struggle with over and under-indulgent behaviors, depending on their moods and company. They can seek to fill emotional holes with food, tobacco, alcohol, or drugs, or they can seek to control emotions through self-imposed regulations on any of these.

Some Type Fours might struggle with a lack of physical activity – rather than an addiction to the physical results of exercise, the tendency toward depression makes some Type Fours lethargic and avoidant of exercise. However, the endorphin release and other endocrine effects of exercise can be successful at counteracting some types of depression.

Overcoming Challenges of the Individualist Ennea-Type

It's important that the Individualist take time to get outside their own head. Connecting with others is essential, because if a Type Four personality does not receive feedback from the outside world, they turn inside to feed their need for attention. Conversation, cooperation, and participation in something greater than themselves help them see their place in their community, keeping them balanced and at their best.

Being the Best Individualist

Harness the best aspects of your Individualist Ennea-type and diminish negative traits that emerge under stress. If you're an Individualist, or know someone who is, consider how the following techniques help you unlock and grow the best version of yourself.

Focus on the Positive

Type Four people need to keep their imaginations in check. Deep feelings and creativity can run wild, and they may have to work to dismiss feelings of negativity and reatain positive emotions. By learning to objectively evaluate feelings, rather than be caught in the turmoil of experiencing them, Individualists learn that feelings do not define them. Individualists have difficulty pulling themselves out of an emotional "funk," but positive feelings from connections with others help Individualists remember their own worth.

Type Four people can find joy in creating a routine and scheduling time to reflect, process, and evaluate their emotions and experiences. Expressing gratitude helps Individualists feel more connected to others. Journaling, meditation, and artistic endeavors can teach a Type Four to explore their feelings actively, then set them aside and move forward into new experiences.

Suggestions:

Schedule a daily routine for reflection or a small act of gratitude. Journal. Scrapbook. Paint. Meditate. Practice yoga. Listen to nature sounds or rhythmic beats to relax and release pent-up emotions. Read or listen to poetry. Sketch. Focus on positive emotions, achievements, and love and connection. Spend time with animals or children.

Turn Visualizations into Actions

Although Type Four people can imagine the future they want, they may not put forth the effort into achieving it. Type Four people naturally love to dream, but they may put off acting on their dreams until the time or the mood "is right." The Individualist at their best finds joy in creation and is fulfilled when sharing their thoughts with the world.

Commitment, discipline, and routine help an Individualist not only produce the creations that fuel their individuality, but the structure can give them the freedom to release their emotions in a controlled, practiced way.

Suggestions:

Create a routine for creativity. Schedule time to create with others. Set deadlines on projects and seek accountability from nonjudgmental friends and family. Involve yourself in a mentoring or teaching role. When others don't acknowledge you the way you want, practice not taking it personally.

There are simple things that an Individualist can do to release their inspiring, supportive energy, especially when they give themselves permission to focus their feelings into creative release.

Chapter 12: Enneagram Type 3 -

Theperformer/Achiever

Performers are free thinkers who tend to harbor a deep-seated fear of failure. They often measure success based upon the respect and approval they receive from others. They are image orientated people who can provide an outwardly positive, well groomed appearance despite sometimes feeling completely desperate and negative about their lives. They are great politicians as they instinctively know when to say nothing. They also excel in selling and advertising roles as their posltlvlty and go getting approach tends to attract other people.

Their positive qualities can make them great leaders, but in their drive for success they can sometimes cause resentment and frustration. They will rely on their natural charisma and charm to get them out of these sticky personal relationship difficulties. They are natural talkers and being so optimistic and confident, they believe they could probably sell snow to the Eskimos.

The negative side of their personality type is that they cannot bear any criticism, even if meant constructively. They often interpret being criticized as failing. Being masters of communication, they can easily use sarcasm as a means of putting someone else down. As their primary motivator is a fear of failure, they will be intolerant of any behavior which is socially unacceptable. This can extend to their children's poor table manners, rudeness or boldness. Anything that could potentially reflect badly on them is simply not tolerated.

Are you a performer?

Do you often feel like you are wearing a mask or acting a role? The world sees a confident, go getter whilst you might see someone who is a bit of a failure?

Do you have very few close friends but a number of friendly acquaintances mainly related to your field of work?

Is it difficult for you to relax and just do nothing?

Do you worry about letting people get too close to you in case they see you are in fact a "failure"?

Do you worry that other people you work with will eventually find out that you are not really capable of doing anything right?

Try these simple tips to help restore the positive aspects of your personality type if you are a succeeder:

Allow other people to love the real you not your job or your financial status

Learn to accept yourself - get rid of the mask. Whilst nobody likes a serial moaner, people who are always on top of the world can be difficult to live with too

Try to appreciate your life as it currently stands. Stop waiting for the next pay rise or promotion to enjoy life.

You can learn to channel your negative characteristic of frantic activity into goal setting. Instead of focusing on outer success, use your natural abilities to work for the benefit of everyone's success.

TRIAD: TYPE 3 IS THE CORE TYPE OF THE HEART TRIAD, WITH TYPES 2 AND 4 BEING THE VARIANTS.

Core Belief: the world values winners, so I must avoid failure at all cost. With this core belief, the Three's focus of attention is on whether they are winning or losing, achieving or failing.

Being valued and recognised for their achievements is a strong driver for Threes. This operates below the level of conscious awareness and underlies everything that they do.

With their focus on winning and achieving, Threes have an optimistic outlook to life. They are confident people who believe in themselves and their abilities. Threes can be charming people, who can change their image to suit the environment they are in.

This chameleon-like nature helps them get on in any environment enabling them to succeed wherever they go. Threes are industrious by nature. They work hard and long hours, and you will often find them taking their work home with them, unable to switch off their drive to succeed.

Because winning is everything, they value themselves and others on the level of their achievements. They will proudly display their trophies and symbols of success.

Whilst Threes are the core point of the Heart Triad, the centre for feelings, they are also the most out of touch with their own feelings of all the Heart Triad types. They are so busy striving to achieve that they do not have time for feelings and for self-reflection. In fact, time is money and to be used wisely. They can be very protective of their time and will not allow anyone to waste it.

At their best, you will often find Threes at or near the top of successful organisations. In sport, you will find them as charming winners who will bask in the spotlight, enjoying the respect they have earned through their achievement. But not for long - Threes are only as good as their last triumph, and will be on to achieving their next victory!

Their strong drive to achieve creates the Threes blind spot, the need to be respected by others at all times. At their weakest, if the Threes do not feel they are gaining the respect they deserve they can become very competitive, winning at all cost. In excess, they can become deceptive and vindictive. Image is everything and they will seek to protect their image of success even where the reality is different. To be seen to have failed would be their worst nightmare, and they will seek to preserve their image of success.

Enneagram Type 4 - The Tragic Romantic

Triad: Type 4 is a variant of the core type of the Heart Triad, with Type 3 being the core type.

Core Belief: Others in the world have something that I do not. What is wrong with me?

With this core belief, the Four's focus of attention is on whether they are accepted or rejected. This operates below the level of conscious awareness and underlies everything that they do.

Whilst Twos learned to get love by giving and Threes learned to earn respect by their achievements, Fours learned to feel accepted by being unique and authentic. With this focus, Fours become creative people who need to express their uniqueness. They are drawn to the arts, drama and other forms of self expression. You can also find them in jobs which require new or unique solutions.

Fours are warm and compassionate people, very in touch with their own feelings and able to feel what others are feeling too. Fours are refined people with an interest in aesthetics and quality.

Threes will seek to fit into a crowd and will dress accordingly. Fours will do anything to stand out from the crowd and will dress to do this. You can often spot a Four in a crowd by their unique dress sense.

This drive to be unique can become the Fours blind spot in that they develop a great fear of being ordinary.

Fours can become depressed, self conscious and withdrawn from the world as they feel the pain of being ordinary.

The drive for uniqueness can be exhausting, and however much they succeed, Fours can still feel there is something still wrong with them. This self absorption can make them stubborn and moody, where their concerns are over dramatised and they can attain a reputation of being a 'drama queen'. Fours feel everything very deeply and are often saddened by life.

Fours, in their search for the meaning of life, to understand their feelings and to be understood, have been inspired to create some of the greatest works of art, music, poetry and literature. They have poured their hearts into the creation of these unique masterpieces, sometimes to the extent that there was nothing left for them at the end, having expended all their deepest feelings in the act of creation.

Examples of Fours (real and/or fictional)

Singers Elton John and Kate Bush

Salvador Dali

Meryl Streep in the film The French Lieutenant's Woman

Types 4 tend to see their lives as a kind of tragedy. They tend to be constantly living in the past and feeling that life has somehow passed them by. They fundamentally feel that something is missing as they cannot seem to accept the ordinariness of their everyday lives. However, they do tend to like being the centre of attention.

The Romantic - in the sense of the romantic movement in art (wild, Byronic) is also known as the Individualist, they have clear values and standards and tend to be very sensitive. When this sensitivity is used positively, they are sensible, perceptive people aware of the needs and wants of their fellow human beings. They make very loyal friends and show great compassion for other people.

They make great teachers as they have the ability to inspire others, even to greatness.

But when used negatively, this sensitivity translates into highly strung, touchy people who can be very difficult to live with. They can be quick to delegate responsibility for everything including their own lives as they get easily bored with "normal" things. They want the "romantic dream" but often lose interest when it actually becomes available.

Past relationships become more "perfect" as time passes and the current relationships pale in comparison. They cannot see that their current life would make them happy if they just accepted what they had.

Some questions to ask if you think you may be a four:

Are you locked in the past examining relationships that might have been?

Do you tend to gravitate towards the dramatic side of life - clothes, food, and people?

Do you often experience so many different emotions that you are not sure what you are feeling and become overwhelmed?

Do you suffer a sense of loss or abandonment even when in a close nurturing relationship?

Tips to try to minimize the negative aspects include:

Mourn a past relationship but make sure you can let it go. Stop dwelling on and reinventing the past.

Work on reducing the dramatic tantrums and learn how to control your mood swings.

Recognize the merits of your current life and partner.

Use your sensitivity to help others deal with their pain whilst building a support network to comfort you when you need it.

You can minimize your introspective behavior and feelings of discouragement and concentrate on loving yourself and using your natural abilities to show compassion and help your fellow man.

Chapter 13: The Point Seven Archetype:

The Enthusiast

Everything is a gift – this is what many Sevens believe in. They have a certain Joie de vivre that shines through They're all about pursuing pleasure, but in a positive way. They live for joy and happiness. They're like kids in a candy store.

They tend to keep their options open, so they're pretty adaptable and can typically weather changes and setbacks in a stride. They're the type who's open to endless possibilities. They're always on the lookout for the next adventure. And they don't just daydream about what they could do – they actually actively chase it. That's why they tend to be always on the go.

However, it has a downside -- they sometimes end up trying to do so many things at once. Healthy sevens, on the other hand, are able to focus their talents and skills on worthwhile goals, and become satisfied.

Identifying An Enthusiast

Sevens operate form the Thinking Center. However, this is not always obvious because they can be quite active. They're always in the middle of something.

Dominant Traits

Optimists - Type sevens are the eternal optimists. They are exuberant, focusing on what brings joy, happiness and pleasure to life makes them

Action-Oriented – Sevens are known for their High Octane energy. Healthy sevens don't just dream about going on an adventure – they actually go for it.

Vivacious – Sevens can be brash and bold in the pursuit of their passions. They are spirited and playful.

Adventurous – Sevens are always on the lookout for the next big adventure.

Adaptable – Because sevens like to keep their options open, they can be pretty flexible when needed. They can weather change. Even if faced with something new or unexpected, they can adapt on the fly.

Prospective – Sevens have visionary qualities that allow them to anticipate an exciting future – and they have the practicality to convert that vision to reality.

Restless – Enthusiasts can get bored easily, which is ironic. They also get depressed when faced with repetitive or mundane tasks. They dislike sitting still.

Thinking Patterns

Sevens tend to be anticipatory – they're always thinking about upcoming events and possibilities.

Sevens are gifted at brainstorming. Their minds tend to go from one idea to the next rather quickly. They get off this influx of ideas. However, they might prefer broad overviews over going in-depth regarding a certain topic. They are not your usual studious or academic type although they ARE intelligent. They can be well-read and articulate. And they thrive on being able to share ideas with other.

The mind of a seven is constantly on, which probably plays a role on why they establish connection between concepts fairly quickly. They're creative and inventive -- the kind of person who knows a lot of things because they accumulate knowledge pretty quickly. They are pretty good at just winging it because they can generate ideas on the fly.

They tend to think that their time and energy should only be spent toward things that actually interest them.

Core fears

Sevens' core fears are related to their inner world. They dislike, if not downright fear, being limited. They steer clear of feelings of pain, loss, deprivation, and anxiety as much as they could, and they deal with this by keeping themselves occupied with endless options and the notion of adventure. Sevens use the stimulation they get from anticipating something as a coping mechanism.

Sevens hate being limited or constrained. Not being able to do something they would like to try is the bane of a seven's existence.

Core Desires

What Sevens really want is to maintain their freedom and happiness. They do not like discomfort so they tend to avoid pain and anxiety, and they usually do so through keeping themselves occupied mentally and physically.

They have immense curiosity and they want to experience all there is that life has to offer and their exuberance is contagious.

Challenges That Sevens Face

Sevens have agile minds that allow them to learn things quickly. However, because they tend to develop quite a varied skillset, they may find it difficult to settle on one thing. Sometimes, they do not know what they're supposed to do. They have difficulty in making commitments and making choices that will benefit them and other people. This can manifest in the simplest of things – a seven might find it hard to think about where to eat for lunch when he's right next to a strip mall with a dozen options in restaurants.

And because they did not really struggle in gaining a certain skill, they might to not value the skills they pick up. Healthy sevens, however, have a well-developed sense of versatility and curiosity that propels them to extraordinary achievement.

This actually occurs when a seven is not in touch with the inner guidance of his true nature, something that is common among all types that operate from the thinking center. This problem instills anxiety within the Seven, and they cope with this feeling by keeping their minds occupied with various projects or plans for the futures. They also seek stimulation as a way to cope, constantly moving from one experience to the next.

The seven's their pursuit of pleasure can be uncontrollable. That's why they tend to have an addictive personality, and can get drawn to compulsive behavior such as shopping, or addictions such as drugs and gambling.

Sevens tend to bite more than they can chew because they take on so many things at once – and that isn't always healthy.

Things could get worse as a seven continues down the unhealthy path. The discontent that drives them to chase after more and more things can result to even worse choices. They may feel frustrated, and even enraged that nothing satisfies them, and this can affect their finances and personal relationships, and even their health.

The extent at which a seven tries to distract himself from negative emotions is an indication of how unhealthy he is. These negative emotions could eat at him from the inside and could manifest in anxiety disorders or depressive episodes.

What Sevens Need To Work on

Sevens try to cram as many options and ideas into their mind as possible because they are constantly chasing stimulation. However, this results in one unfortunate thing – they are unable to recognize their heart's true desire. Sometimes, it can get so buried deep within their unconsciousness that they do not become aware of its existence at all.

The basic need of the Enthusiast, therefore, is to feel satisfied. But they have difficulty experiencing contentment because they are so preoccupied with the future. They tend to think that there's always something better just around the corner so they find it hard to focus and pursue their true devotion.

Career Options For Enthusiasts

You probably encounter a lot of Sevens in the workplace. They tend to have successful careers because they are skilled and they know how to promote it. They know how to share ideas and they exude a positive energy, which is why many higher ups love being around them. They thrive on momentum so they will be acting decisively on things they do like. However, they may have difficulty focusing on a single task.

Sevens tend to be in the art field because that way, they get to nurture their need to create something new constantly. That's why many sevens are content creators, musicians, singers, painters, animators, and authors. Their desire to explore new places and their creativity means they can have a good life being a travel writer. They also make good travel agents and photography for the same reason. As a tour guide, they will satisfy their need to meet new people. They can also make great publicists because they know how to promote their own interests and their enthusiasm can be infectious. Sevens will also thrive in industrial design because they're naturally creative and innovative.

Enthusiasts And Relationships

Sevens can be a bit self-centered because of their high opinion of themselves. It's understandable why they feel that way – after all, they can adapt so well and can learn so quickly – they know so many things. However, this can result to difficulty recognizing what other people experience.

In the workplace, Sevens tend to get along well with others who share their optimistic world view. They like to work with people who can keep up with them and appreciate their input. They prefer working with those who also participate in exciting, new events. They are especially great when working alongside people who are consistent. This is because sevens are very good at generating ideas, but have problems with decision making and committing to an idea. Healthy sevens, however, can also work well with another seven because they will recognize the need to be more consistent. They will hold themselves accountable for their work. They may hit a snag in work relationships when they get bored. They have a tendency to leave a task unfinished if it doesn't excite them.

As for the personal side, sevens are enthusiastic (hence the name) and exciting partners and can 'spice up' the life of the more reserved. However, they have difficulty settling down because they may be holding out for "someone better". When in a romantic relationship with another seven who also has the tendency to constantly seek new things and relationships, communication is important. They need to work together in considering how their actions could impact their partners and the relationship dynamics. Communication can be a problem because sevens do not like to acknowledge negative emotions. In addition, they may occasionally fail to listen because in their mind, they're always trying to cook up something.

Interacting With A Seven

Keep your tone upbeat when communicating with a seven. Sevens avoid people who have negative energy, so don't focus on negativity when trying to get them to communicate with them. For example, focus on solutions, and not the problem.

Sevens tend to avoid situations in which they face negative emotions but thrive on making plans so if you highlight what you could do instead of how screwed up something is, they are more likely to stay and contribute. Keep things lighthearted.

The key to working things out with a seven is compromise. Meet them halfway and discuss multiple solutions.

When giving constructive feedback, be supportive and encouraging,

In line with the sevens' need to avoid negative emotions, they also do not respond well when someone is venting their frustrations. So if you're looking for a shoulder to cry on, sevens are not it. They may also have difficulty expressing negative emotions and difficult feelings.

Expect that sevens will be planning new things to do. Just let the fun happen.

Listen to their ideas and let them know you appreciate them.

How To Be Your Best Self As A Seven

Invest in relationships. You can be happy without going from one thing to the next. In fact, being happy with what you have can fill that seemingly endless hole inside you — it's called contentment. However, you can only have it if you can appreciate the present. You don't have to give up on making plans for the future. It's just that the present can be beautiful in its own way too.

Recognize that you will have the propensity to chase instant gratification, which means you could get addicted to something fairly easy. Be mindful of this tendency.

Negative emotions are unpleasant, and it's understandable to want to avoid them. However, they are part of the human experience. Everyone has bad days. It can't be helped, and it's perfectly okay.

Chapter 14: Type Five - The Investigator

Dominant Traits
- **Isolation**
- **Innovation**
- **Perceptive**
- Secretive

General Behavior

The investigatorpersonality type is no different from the concept of investigation. The one thing that sets them apart from everyone else is their curiosity. They live insightful, curious lives and are always trying to figure out something in life. It might be about them, about someone or something they are involved in, but one thing you can be certain about is that they have questions, and they need answers.

To satisfy this objective, they usually have to be creative and innovate. This is the easiest way for them to make sense of things when there are no answers forthcoming. Investigators have a very good imagination, and the pursuit of knowledge drives them to keep searching for answers.

Their search for answers is not just about knowing things, as it is primarily a self-defense mechanism. They understand the importance of being provided with the necessary information, and this helps them become prepared for anything that life throws at them. They believe there will always be risks, as is normal in life, and the best way to counter this threat is to wield as much information as possible.

Having answers to why people do the things they do is pleasing for investigators. However, it is not just about people; it is also about their surroundings. They question things like the presence of minerals in their town: why gold in this town and not the next town?

Because of their pursuit of knowledge, don't expect investigators to settle for anything forced upon them. If you impose doctrines or sanctions on them, they will only want to know why. Why should they abide by them when they are doing okay the way they are? They will push limits, and before they accept something, they might try to experiment with a contrary opinion.

What drives them to seek knowledge to this extent? What value does gaining this much knowledge add to their lives? The idea is not just in collecting the information; it is about collecting useful information that can shield them from their perceived weaknesses and insecurities. Deep down, investigators struggle to fit in with everyone else. They worry that they are not as good as everyone else. Instead of approaching this challenge from a functional perspective from which they could seek ways of improving their skills or any other shortcomings, it is easier for them to lock themselves up in a tiny laboratory in their minds. This is a safe haven for them where they are able to test hypotheses and draw their conclusions about life.

Typical Action Patterns

It is easy to misunderstand investigators because they are private people, and in an overly social society, this desire for privacy is usually mistaken for rejection. When they choose to set themselves apart from everyone else, it is not because they don't want to interact with them, it is simply because they have established certain boundaries that they don't want to be breached.

Boundaries are healthy because they enable you to define the nature and limits of your interactions. A lot of people have faux boundaries, letting their guard down whenever the situation suits them. Others don't bother to establish boundaries in the first place. For such individuals, interacting with investigators can be very difficult because they are quite serious about their limits.

Investigators spend a lot of time alone, but this does not mean they are lonely or loners. It is simply something they do when they need to get in the zone and figure out some answers. Investigators prefer people who approach them to do it thoughtfully and gently. Before you interrupt their space, ask yourself whether the disruption is absolutely necessary. This comes from the fact that they dislike being bothered with very simple things which you could have done without interrupting them.

Interestingly though, they are very good communicators. They prefer people to ask them things for clarity instead of jumping to conclusions. You should never make assumptions about them because in most cases these will be wrong. Of interest to investigators are people who share their enthusiasm about subjects that are dear to them. If you find them contributing to a subject they enjoy, you will have a fulfilling conversation and will probably create an amazing connection. In social interactions, however, they tend to withdraw and keep to themselves until the moment when something of interest to them is up for discussion.

The investigator's view of the world is that it is a cruel place that keeps demanding a lot from them. To counter this, they live minimalist lives and are largely autonomous. They are survivalists, and most of the time they will make do with the bare minimum.

Typical Thinking Patterns

Think of the investigator as your typical villain from most superhero comics. They are armed to the teeth with information and will not hesitate to use it to gain an advantage, even if it seems unfair to others. They believe that everyone else has access to that knowledge, so they see no fuss in knowing as much as they do about people and situations around them. To learn, they have to be observant and, more importantly, train themselves to anticipate your next move.

You will often find an investigator with a notebook, penning down their thoughts, ideas, and experiences. This gives them an avenue to express themselves and immerse themselves in a world they are more comfortable with. Once they are satisfied with the information they have, they are happy to share it with anyone who cares to listen, showing off that they are well-informed.

The act of sharing this information is a subtle way of seeking approval. Deep down, they need verification and someone who can connect with their input and appreciate their competence. The idea that someone looks up to them as a fountain of knowledge fills them with joy.

A definitive feature of investigators is their hunger for accomplishment. This can be observed in how deep they dive into topics or subjects that they are comfortable with. If they don't know something, they will be quiet and let everyone else shine. However, when a topic comes up that they have knowledge of, the depth of that knowledge usually leaves people astounded. Observers will no longer see them as the quiet people who keep to themselves, but a treasure trove of information, very useful information.

Investigators are often uncomfortable in the presence of other people because of their own serious insecurities and self-esteem issues. The only place where they feel comfortable is alone in their minds because they are free from ridicule, rejection, or judgment. They are not impressed by mundane things which e already knows. This is why they go further and seek the unknown. They exist in a world where there is a lot of information, but somehow they feel that they don't belong. Within this world, they find solace by creating an alternate universe in their minds where they can explore, experiment, and be comfortable with the decisions they make.

Investigators are very good at compartmentalizing. Given their appetite for in-depth information, this is the only way they can avoid information overload. They can compartmentalize so well that they only draw on the information they need to suit a specific purpose and disregard all other knowledge.

Typical Feeling Patterns

Self-preservation is one of the strongest traits of investigators. They usually believe the world is a hostile place, where it is better to protect themselves than to be sorry later on. They are very observant and will notice things that most people ignore or fail to notice altogether.

Because they like to collect information, investigators base their decisions on facts. They are inquisitive and will shun subjectivity in favor of objective decision-making. This is one of the benefits of collecting so much information: it gives their arguments a foundation that they can lean back on if an argument arises or if someone refutes their claim. The last thing you want to do is get into an argument with an investigator because they are well versed in the subject matter, so unless you have equally compelling evidence, you will not make any progress.

Someone who makes use of data for decision making like this is an individual who rationalizes feelings and does not just act on things because they feel something. They question those thoughts and emotions so that by the time they make a decision, it is backed by proven evidence. One problem with this approach is that they are often unable to tell the difference between what they feel and what they think. Their brains are always working overtime to understand what goes on around them, which means that the pressure slows them down as the day drags along. The brain has to process a lot of information at once, in the process of which they become lethargic.

This disconnect between their thoughts and emotions manifests in different ways. One of these is that at times, investigators are unable to identify with their emotions. Often, investigators choose to withdraw from occasions where they might be forced to confront their emotions so that they do not have to embrace the pain. If they can reason out of it, they will do so.

In interactions, people often feel that investigators are cold, something felt especially by people who feel deeply about the things that go on around them. They can come across as people who show no emotion and don't appear to be bothered by many things. Their attention is often focused on preparing for potential disruption, enhancing their intellectual understanding and finding out as much as they can about other people's agendas before they meet.

How to Improve Your Life

You need to realize the difference between the real world and your imaginary world. At times, you withdraw from the true experiences of your life and focus on other people. Recognize the fact that you have a beautiful mind. Your creativity is amazing, but don't get carried away and lose sight of the physicality of your existence. Enjoy your life.

Trust is a difficult proposition. You are not the only person who struggles with trusting people. Given the nature of the world, as it is, trust does not come easily to many. You will often focus on self-preservation over everything else and, while it is okay to protect yourself, you must also realize that you cannot avoid conflict. Some conflicts are necessary, and they help to build your character. Instead of isolating yourself, embrace these as learning points in your life. This might help you learn how to have a healthy conflict without feeling burdened.

As you engage in different projects, remind yourself why you are working on them, and whether their objectives align with your personal objectives. Projects and interactions that do not add value to your confidence, improve your life or self-esteem are a waste of time. They might distract you from achieving your potential.

Find healthy ways of rejuvenating. Your mind is always on high alert, and this can be frustrating as you try to preempt the next move someone will make. Take yourself out of the equation from time to time and allow yourself room to relax and enjoy the beauty of life. If you can do this without indulging in alcohol or any other potentially harmful behavior, you will be making serious progress in life.

Chapter 15: Find A New Job With Enneagram And Become A Great Leader

Finding the best job for you to suit who you are at your base core can be important to your thriving as an individual. Stop to consider the amount of sleeping versus waking hours that we each have in any given day, and then factor in how many of those waking hours we spend at work, or thinking about work. The majority of us spend a good portion of those waking hours focused on a single aspect of our lives... work.

Using the Enneagram system of personality typing can make a big difference in how we grow as individuals when we use it to help us discover the type of work we can excel in. Some may even find themselves surprised because that is where they have been all along, or... maybe they hadn't considered such a change in employment would bring the potential of such benefit to us by making us utilize our strengths.

Job Typing

Type Ones:

With their continual striving for perfection comes a great deal of problem-solving abilities, coupled with strong attention to detail. Ones like a great deal of structure and if it isn't already in place, they are quite capable of creating it. They have good memory retention skills and rarely make mistakes. They do not do well in positions that are chaotic or requires flexible hours.

Possible Career Choices for Ones:

Executive (including entrepreneurial), Lawyer (or choices in the legal profession such as Paralegal), Management, Financial Broker or Planner, Computer Programmer, Accountant, Urban Planning/Home Design

Type Twos:

Twos are definitely the helpers and givers of the Enneagram, but to work in a field directly helping others could push them over the edge. They need to work in a field more indirectly supporting and helping others in order to thrive. Any job that takes advantage of their warmth and caring, or causes them to have to deny or turn others down, would have a devastating effect on a Two.

Possible Career Choices for Twos:

Stay-at-Home Parent hits the top of the Twos list, as does Teacher (especially for younger ages), Doctor, Therapist, Fire Fighter, Paramedic, Bartender (or Waiter/Waitress), Wedding Planner, Caterer, Retail Sales or a Sales Rep, Graphic or Fashion Design, Publicist, Advice Columnist

Type Threes:

Threes love to be around influential people - the more important, the better. They want to love their job, like anyone else and be good at it, but it is more important for them to get recognition for their contributions than what the actual job itself might be. That being said, they do enjoy positions that are considered by society to be more "successful." They enjoy the competition and want a clear-cut ladder to climb to show their achievements as they happen. Any kind of career that involves self-employment, because there are no real clear-cut ways to advance, and no one else around to provide them accolades, are choices Threes should avoid in general.

Possible Career Choices for Threes:

Salesperson, Personal or Executive Assistant (especially to someone perceived as important or influential), Attorney, Agent (of most any kind... Sports, Literary, Travel, or even Insurance!), News Journalist, Producer, Political Activist, Inspirational Speaker and/or Writer, Performer/Entertainer. Life and/or Business Coach

Type Fours:

Fours excel in the deep examination of emotions, and in anything that involves creativity or creatively expressing themselves. They fare far better in a relaxed, flexible environment than they do one with any kind of rigid structure or routine.

Possible Career Choices for Fours:

Yoga or Dance Instructor, Masseuse, Holistic Health Practitioner, Life Coach, Relationship/Couples Counseling, Psychotherapist, Crisis-Line Operator, Actor, Musician, Artist, Writer, Designer, Hair Stylist, Tattooist

Type Fives:

Fives will definitely thrive in any position that offers science, technology, and/or research. They are not your normal mainstream workers, because they tend to be far more cerebral than most and will not do well in any positions where they can be chastised or criticized for something that is not their fault.

Possible Career Choices for Fives:

Anything involving technology (from engineering of any kind all the way to game and app design and development), manager, Risk Management Advisor (especially financial), Astronomer, Physicist, College Professor, Researcher (of any kind), Technical Support, Analyst, Environmental Planner

Type Sixes:

Sixes are highly adaptable but cautious. They lean toward meticulousness and are great team players, but they are also great worriers. They try to think ahead and plan for every eventuality. They far prefer structure and stability, because it leaves them in a comfort zone of knowing exactly where they're at and what's expected of them. They would not fare well in positions where they have to take risks but would do well in positions where she could turn the negative concerns into something positive.

Possible Career Choices for Sixes:

Paralegal, Analyst, Actuarial Scientist, Health and Safety Inspector, Public Notary, Security Guard, Teacher or College Professor, Activist, Writer, Comic Artist,

Stand-up Comedian, Technical Support, Child-Care Worker

Conclusion

We all have understood at this point that emotional intelligence is the very powerful ability to manage our own emotions, as well as others'. We have appreciated how this ability can only impact all of our relationships positively. May none of us ever neglect to sustain the mind and body with healthy habits. Emotionally intelligent habits affect how we perceive situations, how situations evoke thoughts, and ultimately, how our thoughts contribute to how we feel and express our reactions.

Taking proactive steps in keeping your emotions under control will only help you in the best ways in all aspects of your life. This elusive ability of regulating one's feelings will allow you to manage your emotions in stressful conditions and develop your instincts, instead of always succumbing to the aggravatingly typical fight, flight, or freeze responses. If you take the brave steps down this beaten path of building your EI, you are assured of nothing but intelligent, balanced, and well-informed decisions throughout your life.

I cannot reiterate it enough, how important a highly developed EI is to one's career growth. We've now learned that a majority of hiring businesses actually utilize EI-based assessment instruments in recruitment and in evaluating existing manpower for potential for success.

If you are eyeing more responsibilities or a promotion to an actual leadership role (which comes with more responsibilities, by default) at work, your EI levels will likely be a key determinant. EI is essential for leadership responsibilities as higher positions typically translate more people reporting to you.

Or you could be at a point in your life when you are starting to yearn for that relationship that will see you to the twilight of your life or just more meaningful relationships, in general.

You've also possibly suspected at least once that you could use some help with how you behave under pressure. You might have made a string of decisions you regret 'till now. Whatever crossroad you are at right now, what matters most is that you are at a turning point. Moments in a person's life when he or she decides to undertake a definitive change is always good. Though you will not always be able to predict all outcomes, change is, at the very least, the right step into a direction.

www.ingramcontent.com/pod-product-compliance
Lightning Source LLC
Chambersburg PA
CBHW072012070526
44583CB00015B/1444